CLEAR
CONSCIENCE

A CATHOLIC GUIDE TO VOTING

WITH A FOREWORD BY KEVIN CIEPLY
PRESIDENT AND DEAN OF AVE MARIA SCHOOL OF LAW

AN ASCENSION GUIDE

ASCENSION

West Chester, Pennsylvania

Ascension
PO Box 1990
West Chester, PA 19380
1-800-376-0520
ascensionpress.com

Cover design: Rosemary Strohm

Printed in the United States of America

20 21 22 23 24 5 4 3 2 1

ISBN 978-1-950784-43-1

CONTENTS

Foreword

I'm not sure I even knew what the word *jurisprudence* meant as I sat in my first class with Professor Charlie Rice at Notre Dame. If I did, I know I didn't understand it.

Today, I look back on that class and still draw much inner strength from it. At a critical time in my life, it set my moral compass. I still see Professor Rice in my mind's eye: chiseled facial features, Marine hair-cut, standing strong and exhibiting an unusual degree of inner confidence and peace. Professor Charlie Rice was larger than life.

The most important lesson I learned from him was the first precept of natural law: "Good is to be done and pursued, and evil is to be avoided."

This book seeks to help each of us seek good and avoid evil.

It is timely. The world seems to be coming apart at the seams— COVID-19, racial unrest, economic uncertainty, all under a growing loss of faith. Domestically, we are blessed to live in the greatest and most free nation on earth. And yet everything is politicized, and hurtful exchanges of words pit friends, colleagues, and brothers and sisters against one another.

Perhaps, there has never been a more critical time in our lives to exercise our political freedom to vote; but perhaps there has also never been a more confusing period.

The stakes are high—the future of our children and our children's children.

So how do we vote? Is there a way to rationally measure the issues and candidates to ensure that we really are seeking good and avoiding evil?

Clear Conscience: A Catholic Guide to Voting helps us answer those important questions and guides us as we approach local, state, and national elections. It begins with a primer on the meaning of politics and the law. It draws on Scripture, natural law, the *Catechism of the Catholic Church*, and papal teachings, such as the words of St. John Paul II. It not only provides a foundation for us to stand on as we cast our ballots—that is, a foundation that brings our faith, our patriotism, our morals, and our sense of fairness and justice together; it also builds on that foundation to provide specific guidance on contemporary issues, bridging our will to do good with the best policies to accomplish it.

This book helps us navigate the most contentious, confusing, and perilous issues of the day, such as the erosion of patriotism and the nuclear family. It analyzes and provides concrete guidance to issues such as immigration, poverty, guns, and the environment. And of course, it provides the principles that undergird our Catholic Faith's non-negotiable position on life issues.

What this book does not do is tell you who to vote for or against, and what issues and policies you should or should not support. Indeed, my favorite chapter is Chapter Eight, "Prudential Judgment." It starts off with the imperative that Catholics can never promote anything that violates the inherent dignity of the human person—and then quickly moves to the theme of the chapter—that the Church "leaves the majority of policy questions up to our sound judgment."

If, as I suspect, you thirst for authenticity and congruency and sacredness in your life, how you vote plays a significant role in fulfilling that quest. As faithful Catholics, we have a duty to exercise our right to vote in ways that harmonize faith and reason. We have a responsibility to our families and the future of our country to seek good and avoid evil. This book will help you tremendously in that endeavor.

Kevin Cieply
President and Dean
Ave Maria School of Law

Introduction

This book does not tell you who to vote for or what position to take on each complex political issue that candidates and pundits debate every election season.

And as it happens, neither does the Catholic Church.

As you will discover in the following chapters, the Church is not a political party, and its teachings are not a political platform. The Church has authority in political matters, but only when politics invades its turf.

That turf is in the realm of the eternal. The unchanging truths about the dignity of mankind and the meaning of human life.

TAKING RESPONSIBILITY FOR OUR POLITICS

Outside of those teachings, the Catholic Church leaves us free to discern what is best in our political environment and even to arrive at diverse political conclusions on all but just a few immutable "life" issues.

This is why no Catholic priest or bishop can order us to do or not to do anything based on our convictions about certain political issues, such as how best to address climate change. This is also why Catholics do not need permission from our spiritual leaders before we take action to defend our religious liberty when we feel it is under threat. The Church's leaders can offer opinions on such specific political questions, of course, but their authority on such issues lies in the validity of their reasoned arguments, just like any other Catholic. Otherwise, no community initiative on many important issues could be undertaken without Catholics first obtaining permission from their pastor or bishop of each diocese.

The *Catechism of the Catholic Church* (CCC), however, is clear in this regard:

> It is not the role of the Pastors of the Church to intervene directly in the political structuring and organization of social life. This task is part of the vocation of *the lay faithful, acting on their own initiative with their fellow citizens*. Social action can assume various concrete forms. It should always have the common good in view and be in conformity with the message of the Gospel and the teaching of the Church. It is the role of the laity "to animate temporal realities with Christian commitment, by which they show that they are witnesses and agents of peace and justice." (CCC 2442, emphasis added)

As any priest will tell you, the Church *needs* Catholics "in the pews" to act independently in the realm of politics.

In practical terms, given the hierarchical nature of the Church, much of the necessary agility to act with urgency when needed would be lost if Catholics needed to obtain clerical permission before acting as they prudentially discern they should in the political sphere.

As the *Catechism* states,

> Since, like all the faithful, lay Christians are entrusted by God with the apostolate by virtue of their Baptism and Confirmation, they have the right and duty, individually or grouped in associations, to work so that the divine message of salvation may be known and accepted by all men throughout the earth. ... Their activity in ecclesial communities is

so necessary that, for the most part, *the apostolate of the pastors cannot be fully effective without it.* (CCC 900, emphasis added)

ACTING WITH A CLEAR CONSCIENCE

The responsibility of Catholics, then, regarding political life is certainly great. By the same token, though, taking a direct hand in the "political structuring and organization of social life" means that we had better know what we are doing.

After all, the policies we promote and the candidates for whom we vote can have enormous effects in the lives of many. Going about politics haphazardly would amount to being careless with our neighbors' lives. We need to approach politics and voting with a *clear conscience.* The only way to do this is by obtaining a *clear understanding* of the unwavering truths the Christian faith teaches about human beings and society.

In **Chapter One**, we will discuss the Church's embrace of the best of Greco-Roman political thought. We will see that human reason is a legitimate and God-given means of discovering what is best for us and our neighbors—and that politics is not some frivolous human invention; rather, it is as natural to us as the loving bond between members of a family. Finally, we will present the true purpose of politics—which is to make us "happy." (Amazing, but true.)

In **Chapter Two**, we will discover how the Church inherited and perfected the political principles of the Old Testament. God's revelation to his Chosen People gives us everything human reason has to offer and more. We will see how sin poses a primordial threat to our fulfillment and happiness, which is why God gave us eternal laws to free us.

Chapter Three presents the "political miracle" of Jesus. The Church he founded adopted and "Christianized" the best of ancient Jewish and Greco-Roman culture and shared it with the entire world. The result? The invention of the notion of inherent human rights, a world in which governments are held accountable for how they treat God's children.

Chapter Four introduces the concept of natural law, which is the law that God wrote into the fabric of all of created reality. We cannot violate the natural law without serious consequences, any more than we can violate the law of gravity by "flying" out of a second-story window without suffering serious injuries. In this chapter, we will also discuss "positivism," the theory that political leaders can ignore natural law whenever they see fit. Positivism, in one form or another, is responsible for some of the worst atrocities in human history—atrocities that highlight the importance of Catholics like you speaking up boldly on behalf of the natural law.

In **Chapter Five**, we see why the Church has always embraced patriotism as a Christian virtue. Patriotism, though, can be twisted into a chauvinistic and unthinking national pride or a cringing obedience to the whims of demagogic leaders. True patriotism is based in nature. Just as we are called to honor our parents and our families, we owe our nation a special honor—because it is *our* nation.

In **Chapter Six**, we discuss the pitfalls of political power. When human beings have a great deal of power, they have a tendency to abuse it and end up hurting others. Historically, even leaders of the Church were overcome by this temptation when they found themselves with temporal and military power over lands and regions. We know that *might* does not make *right*. In fact, it is more likely to make us wrong.

Chapter Seven presents a thorough analysis of what a government owes its citizens, and what we as citizens owe our government. We have a place in our political environment, and if we abandon our role, we can expect the government to begin to fail or, just as bad, try to take over the role we abdicated. Big government is not equipped to do well what we, our families, and our community are meant to do.

On a similar note, **Chapter Eight** helps us see the moral questions that we, as Christian citizens, must figure out for ourselves. The Church leaves many political issues in the realm of "prudential judgment"—that is, the realm of personal conscience. This means that we must be all the more serious about thinking clearly and conscientiously about our media consumption, our public witness, and our vote.

Starting with **Chapter Nine**, we will begin a Catholic "guided tour" of specific political issues, the first being war. Then, in **Chapters Ten through Sixteen**, we will proceed through a discussion of guns, poverty, immigration, racial injustice, the environment, human life, and human sexuality—and the implications each of these topics has on our political involvement.

Finally, in the **Epilogue**, we will discuss the immeasurable importance of religious liberty. In fact, without religious liberty, nothing in this book amounts to anything.

WHY EVERY CATHOLIC SHOULD READ THIS BOOK

As Americans and Catholics, we are blessed with a great political heritage.

We take for granted that all human beings have dignity and worth. We believe that torture, enslavement, and oppression are unacceptable. We accept that even the lowliest among us have rights—and that it is immoral to violate those rights. We even believe that violations of such rights should be illegal.

We may think these ideas are obvious or even cliché. Actually, they are *brilliant.* Throughout world history—and even in some places today—relatively few nations have known and embraced these principles and put them into practice.

Sadly, when it comes to world politics, abuse and corruption are more the norm than the exception—a fact that should make us see our own political order as all the more precious. What is more, our political heritage has been hard won. It has been carefully distilled by ingenious, courageous, and holy people over the course of millennia.

Think of our political heritage as a family heirloom, lovingly maintained by countless generations of our forebears. They polished it, kept it safe, and defended it from burglars. Many sacrificed their lives for it to ensure that we would possess it. It is now up to us to take ownership of this legacy—and hand it down intact to future generations.

A first step is simply to learn and understand the political legacy we enjoy today.

PART ONE
PRINCIPLES

CHAPTER ONE
What Is Politics?

It has been said that human beings are "political animals." What does this mean, though?

We will start with the word "politics" itself, which comes to us from the ancient Greeks, whose name for its city-states was *polis*. A city-state was simply a city and the area around it that it governed, such as Athens or Sparta in ancient Greece.

One of the most influential Greek philosophers was Aristotle (385–323 BC). His writings on the topic of politics are simply entitled *Politics*—meaning, roughly, "the work of running a city-state." In the first book of *Politics*, Aristotle establishes that the state is "natural" to us rather than something to be avoided. By "natural," he means arising from our nature as human beings.

Just as the family is an "association established by nature," so is the village a cooperation of several families working together for their collective welfare. Following the same logic, Aristotle continues,

> When several villages are united in a single complete community, large enough to be nearly or quite self-sufficing, the state comes into existence. ... And therefore, if the earlier forms of society are natural, so is the state.[1]

He adds, "For [the state] is the end of them, and the nature of a thing is its end." And he concludes that "the state is a creation of nature, and that man is by nature a political animal." Let us consider what this means.

THE WORLD IS *INTELLIGIBLE*

What does it mean for the state to be the "end" of "earlier forms of society"? What does Aristotle mean by "the nature of a thing"? How can the state be a creation of nature?

For Aristotle, the world in which we live is intelligible and orderly; it is not meaningless or chaotic. We can understand things, and—in principle—the mysteries of the universe can be solved.

The way we understand a given category of things is by finding out what makes it unique. What makes a plant different from a rock? What makes a human being different from an animal?

Every kind of thing in the universe has what Aristotle calls a "specific difference," which gives it its identity and purpose. One word Aristotle uses for that identity and purpose is "end." Another is "nature," as in "human nature."

The words "species" and "specific" have the same root. Aristotle uses "specific differences" to identify the nature of each "species" of things.

For the human species, the specific difference is our intellect or mind. This is something no other creature possesses, and it enables us to control and discipline ourselves, rather than merely act on instinct.

Animals simply act on instinct to fulfill their natures, and they have no need to "think" about it. Human beings, though, have intellects and the unique ability to choose. We are called to choose an excellence beyond our impulses and whims. This excellence, according to Aristotle, is virtue.

HAPPINESS IS THE FULFILLMENT OF HUMAN NATURE

The virtuous life is the only path to the fulfillment of our nature—our "end;" that is, the meaning and purpose of life.

Aristotle acknowledges that virtue is more difficult to live than vice. For him, virtue is the "middle way" between the many extremes of vice. In Aristotle's view, the opposite of cowardice is actually another vice—rashness. The virtue in relation to cowardice is the "middle" way—courage—which lies halfway between cowardice and rashness.

That is why living the virtues can be difficult. Doing so requires carefully navigating between the extremes of vice. Nothing, though, is more worthwhile than living virtuously. Why? Because pursuing virtue is the only way to true happiness—which Aristotle calls the purpose ("end") of life.

Elsewhere, Aristotle teaches that our happiness depends on the exercise of reason. Ultimately, he says, happiness is an "activity of the soul," which he identifies as contemplation. But to enjoy this, we need material security:

> Being a man, one will also need external prosperity;
> for our nature is not self-sufficient for the purpose
> of contemplation, but our body also must be healthy
> and must have food and other attention.[2]

While it is certainly possible to be good in times of adversity, oppression and danger can get in the way of living a good life. The political philosopher Russell Kirk puts it this way: "A truly happy life, Aristotle argues in his *Ethics*, is an existence of goodness, free from impediments—that is, reasonably secure from poverty, sickness, and restrictions."[3]

In other words, our best chance at being good—and therefore happy—is to live in a state that protects our liberty from impediments to virtue. We need that freedom from the fears of starvation, violence, or working to the point of exhaustion.[4]

A GOOD GOVERNMENT HONORS HUMAN NATURE

While Aristotle's political commentary is rich and sophisticated, if there is a single Aristotelian contribution to political thought that remains with us to this day, it is this: *There is a human nature, and the state (i.e., the government) ought to honor it and certainly never violate it.*

It is impossible to overstate the value of this one piece of Greek wisdom. It says, in short, that the purpose of the *polis*, and of politics, aligns with the purpose and meaning of human life: The ideal state facilitates virtue and happiness in its citizens.

CHAPTER TWO

The Fall and the Law

As we have seen, the ancient Greek philosophers contributed immensely to the development of modern political thought. They arrived at their conclusions solely by the light of human reason. The other group that has had a significant influence on modern political life, the Jews, however, derived their politics from the Law given them by God.

Of course, this does not imply that Jewish political thought was too lofty or, perhaps to some, even considered *unreasonable* because it involved "theology"; it was based on their *experience* as a people—namely, their experience of the living God and his revelation to them.

As recorded in the books of Genesis and Exodus, they were liberated from the grueling yoke of slavery through the direct intervention of the Lord so that they could enter into a covenant relationship with him. In this covenant, they were bound to observe the Law given them by God through Moses.

Their story marked them with a profound belief in the importance of the moral law, a strong sense of the dignity of the oppressed among them, and a fierce readiness to stand up for what was right.

CREATION AND THE FALL

Genesis, the first book of the Torah, reveals that our first parents, Adam and Eve, were created by God with immeasurable dignity—in God's own image and likeness (see Genesis 1:26-27). They were given "dominion" over all other created things (see Genesis 1:28). As the *Catechism* puts it, the book of Genesis teaches us that the whole universe is "destined for and addressed to man, himself created in the 'image of God' and called to a personal relationship with God" (CCC 299).

The story, however, soon takes a dark turn. In an act of disobedience, Adam and Eve sin against God. The results were catastrophic. They lost the grace-filled relationship with their Creator and were expelled from paradise. Now exposed to the elements and all the dangers of the natural world, they are forced to hunt and labor for their food and shelter in order to avoid starvation, injury, and death.

In addition to these new dangers, they soon discover another terrible consequence of the Fall. They and their descendants now have an inclination toward sin. We see this in the story of their firstborn sons, Cain and Abel. In a fit of rage, Cain murders his brother.

The *Catechism* states,

> After that first sin [of Adam], the world is virtually inundated by sin. There is Cain's murder of his brother Abel and the universal corruption which follows in the wake of sin. Likewise, sin frequently manifests itself in the history of Israel. ... Scripture and the Church's Tradition continually recall the presence and universality of sin in man's history: "What Revelation makes known to us is confirmed by our own experience. For when man looks into his own heart he finds that he is drawn towards what is wrong and sunk in many evils which cannot come from his

good creator. Often refusing to acknowledge God as his source, man has also upset the relationship which should link him to his last end, and at the same time he has broken the right order that should reign within himself as well as between himself and other men and all creatures." (CCC 401)

Human beings are now a danger to one another.

POLITICAL CONSEQUENCES OF THE FALL: THE LAWS OF MEN

Despite humanity's sinfulness, in his loving kindness, God nonetheless makes covenants with Adam's descendants. Abraham, Isaac, and Jacob all receive visitations and promises from the Lord. The essential condition of the Fall remained, however.

This is seen in the book of Exodus, which begins with the enslavement of the Israelites in Egypt. As Genesis ends, the Israelites were saved from famine by Joseph, one of Jacob's sons, who had become a powerful political figure in Egypt. After Joseph passes away, though, "there arose a new king over Egypt, *who did not know Joseph*" (Exodus 1:8, emphasis added). Under the direction of this new Pharaoh, the Egyptians "set taskmasters over [the Israelites] to afflict them with heavy burdens" (Exodus 1:11).

Still, the Pharaoh fears the Israelites' numbers and strength. So he issues a terrible command: He orders Hebrew midwives to kill all male children. However, the narrative tells us the midwives "feared God, and did not do as the king of Egypt commanded them, but let the male children live. ... So God dealt well with the midwives; and the people multiplied and grew very strong. And because the midwives feared God he gave them families" (Exodus 1:17, 20-21).

In these first few verses of Exodus we can already see a theme developing, one that will repeat itself throughout Jewish history: Human governments are as unreliable as fallen human nature itself.

In the long run, Joseph's role as a close advisor to the Pharaoh did not protect his people from becoming enslaved. A new Pharaoh comes to the throne, the political winds shift, and the Hebrews lose political favor and become slaves. In the story of the midwives, though, we see a silver lining to the theme of the fickleness of political power.

THE ONLY KIND OF LAW THAT SETS US FREE

The eternal, unchanging will of God—that is, the natural moral law—grants legitimacy to human laws. It is through the light of the natural moral law that we can determine whether a particular law is just or unjust.

Ultimately, an important political principle flows from this truth: Governments must be limited in their actions by the framework of the moral law, forbidding themselves and their agents to violate it.

Egypt at the time of the Exodus, and for the four centuries preceding it, provides Scripture's premier example of the alternative kind of government: Rule by the whims of fallen man, in this case, the corrupt and arrogant Pharaoh.

At the end of the first chapter of Exodus, the Hebrews' suffering at the hands of the Egyptians is still far from over. Seeing what the midwives have done, Pharaoh orders his men to abduct and murder all the Israelites' male children. Then, we learn that one of these infants is saved and becomes Moses, whom God will raise up to lead the Israelites from bondage. In the end, Moses is the most important person in the Torah because he is the one who receives the Law of God.

Torah itself means "law" (or "doctrine," "guidance," or "teaching"). For the Hebrews, nothing could be more imperative than obedience to it.

God uses Moses, and a series of great miracles, to free the Israelites from slavery in Egypt. After their liberation, God enters into a covenant with the Israelites and gives them his Law through Moses, beginning with the Ten Commandments.

1. I am the LORD your God: you shall not have strange gods before me.

2. You shall not take the name of the LORD your God in vain.

3. Remember to keep holy the LORD's Day.

4. Honor your father and your mother.

5. You shall not kill.

6. You shall not commit adultery.

7. You shall not steal.

8. You shall not bear false witness against your neighbor.

9. You shall not covet your neighbor's wife.

10. You shall not covet your neighbor's goods.[5]

The Lord did not just provide them with the Ten Commandments, however. In the next three books—Leviticus, Numbers, and Deuteronomy—Moses goes on to instruct the Israelites in hundreds of other laws for ordering their everyday lives as God's people.

To modern ears, this might seem somewhat contradictory. Why would God free the Israelites from slavery only to bind them with a strict adherence to a set of laws?

The answer is the central political idea found in the Torah: For the Jews, it is human laws—like the laws of Egyptian Pharaohs—that can enslave us. Only the Law of God can free us from enslavement to sin and tyranny. As we saw at the beginning of the book of Exodus, the laws of men are fickle, ever changing, and prone to becoming nothing more than tools that powerful men use to impose their will on others.

This principle, of course, remains with us to this day. In the United States, we are blessed not only to be free from oppressive laws but from lawlessness itself. Why? Due to our society's historical acceptance of the moral law embodied in the Ten Commandments. If this were not the case, we would not be free from the threat of being thrown out on the street in our old age (fourth commandment), our neighbors might abduct members of our family (ninth commandment), others might steal our property (seventh commandment), people might ruin our reputation and career by libel (eighth commandment), or even take our bodies by force, under threat of murder (fifth commandment) or for their own pleasure (sixth commandment).

For the ancient Hebrews, the Law was not only a path to salvation from misery but also the surest means to protect those who were the most susceptible to oppression. The Jews understood that they were free only due to the intervention of the Lord, who undeservedly frees them from slavery in Egypt and keeps them free by obedience to his Law.

Due to their four centuries of bondage in Egypt, ancient Israelites could easily relate to those who were oppressed. It is no coincidence that the Torah explicitly mentions the oppressed in the Law. God tells his people,

> You shall not wrong a stranger or oppress him, for you were strangers in the land of Egypt. You shall not afflict any widow or orphan. If you do afflict them, and they cry out to me, I will surely hear their cry. (Exodus 22:21-23)

The Law given to Moses and handed on from generation to generation among the Jews was their only protection against the dangers and hostilities of the fallen world. It is the eternal Law, the unchanging Law, and the Law authored by God himself that gives us the freedom for which we have been created.

CHAPTER THREE
The Good News

Like the Israelites of the Old Testament, Christians are inheritors of a concrete history. Our inheritance includes not only the writings of the New Testament but the intellectual riches of accumulated human wisdom.

This is because the Catholic Faith has always been marked by a readiness to *adapt* itself to various peoples and cultures. From its inception, the Church has incorporated elements of the cultures in which it has preached and ministered, including elements of their political philosophies that are compatible with the gospel. This is especially true of Greek and Roman political thought.

CHRISTIANITY BRINGS THE LAW FROM ISRAEL TO ALL NATIONS

In Jesus Christ, "the Word became flesh and dwelt among us" (John 1:14). The Second Person of the Trinity took on human nature. He suffered and died for all humanity. He then rose from the dead and instructed his apostles to "make disciples of all nations, baptizing them in the name of the Father and of the Son and of the Holy Spirit" (Matthew 28:19).

Armed with the saving message of the gospel, Christians set
out into the world, filled with zeal to accomplish the mission
given them by Jesus. For the first few centuries of the Church,
however, Christians were politically oppressed by the Roman
Empire, even as their faith spread like wildfire throughout
the known world.

Even from the Church's earliest days, however, we can already
see the development of uniquely Christian political insights—
in particular, a universal call to love for others that would
reshape Western political philosophy forever. As a famous
second-century text describes Christians,

> [They] are distinguished from other men neither
> by country, nor language, nor the customs which
> they observe. For they neither inhabit cities of their
> own, nor employ a peculiar form of speech, nor
> lead a life which is marked out by any singularity.
> ... But, inhabiting Greek as well as barbarian cities,
> according as the lot of each of them has determined,
> and following the customs of the natives in respect
> to clothing, food, and the rest of their ordinary
> conduct, they display to us their wonderful and
> confessedly striking method of life.[6]

This method of life, the author continues, is that "they love
all men."

Later in this same letter, the author makes clear Christians
are not "advocates of any merely human doctrines." Rather,
"God has assigned them this illustrious position, which it
were unlawful for them to forsake."

In other words, the Christian way of life is not a product
of philosophy or human reason but of *revelation*—God's
communication of himself to humanity. That said, since God
is the author of both revelation and reason, the contents of
the Faith are always *reasonable*.

Note that the author says it would be "unlawful" for Christians to live in any way other than the way they do. This reference to the law is a clear reference to the revealed Law of God. In this regard, the early Christians are seen to resemble the ancient Jews more than the Romans and Greeks among whom they live, for the entire Jewish way of life was rooted in obedience to the Torah, the Law of Moses.

The early Christians, though, did not distinguish themselves from their neighbors in language, diet, and dress, as did the Jews. In addition, unlike the Jews of their time, the early Christians accepted the laws and customs of the nations in which they lived and identified as citizens of those states.

For the ancient Jews, the Law was not only a personal ethic but a "national constitution." It ordered every aspect of society and kept it from devolving into the chaos and barbarism to which humanity is susceptible due to original sin.

THE LAW HAS BECOME A PERSON

With the coming of Jesus, something extraordinary happened: the Torah itself—and God the Lawgiver—became man and dwelt among his people. This led to what Pope Benedict XVI calls a "new family" and a "new Israel." While the Torah gave God's people a clear social order, a framework "for just politics and for daily life," Jesus' coming brings something more:

> Discipleship of Jesus offers no politically concrete program for structuring society. ... In Jesus' case it is not the universally binding adherence to the Torah that forms the new family. Rather, it is adherence to Jesus himself, to his Torah.[7]

Some Jews saw the political ramifications of Jesus' message as a threat to the social order. Jesus' earliest followers, all of whom were Jews, embraced these ramifications as part of the fulfillment and ultimate meaning of the Law.

The Old Testament promised that God's salvation would one day come to all nations. "We hear that the boundaries will fall and that the God of Israel will be acknowledged and revered by all the nations as their God, as the one God."[8] As Benedict XVI continues,

> So ... what has Jesus brought? ... He has brought the God of Israel to the nations, so that all the nations now pray to him and recognize Israel's Scriptures as his word, the word of the living God. He has brought the gift of universality, which was the one great definitive promise to Israel and the world.[9]

Jesus Christ is the Torah made flesh. Recognizing Jesus as the Messiah—as the fulfillment of the Law of the Old Testament, who brings salvation to "all nations"—is what sets the Christians apart from those who do not accept him as such. Jesus' commandment to love others—that is, *everyone*—in the same selfless way he has loved us is revolutionary.

It is this universality that gives Christians the distinctive way of life praised in the Epistle to Diognetus: "They love all men." This way of life is made possible only by following Jesus, who commands it. Jesus also provided the means to live this way—which is a relationship with himself, which brings his grace to live according to this new "law of love" for all.

THE LAW OF CHRIST SURPASSES CIVIL LAWS

What does this Christian "love for all" have to do with politics? It compels Christians to live and work fully within the political arrangements of secular states. They are free from the ordinary ways of the world, which looks out only for the welfare of one's own people, nation, ethnicity, or religion. As the author of the Epistle to Diognetus tells us, "Every foreign land is to them as their native country ... and every land of their birth as a land of strangers. ... They obey the prescribed laws, and at the same time surpass the laws by their lives."[10]

According to Benedict XVI, there is a profound political consequence to Christ's coming, which he calls an "extremely important process whose full scope was not grasped until modern times" and "an epoch-making event in world history that has not occurred as such in any other culture." His coming releases "the concrete political and social order ... from the directly sacred realm, from theocratic legislation" and transfers it "to the freedom of man."[11]

Jesus commands his followers to love all men. He also commands us to approach politics differently. By extending himself to all nations, he calls us to recognize the validity of human political pursuits among all free peoples and nations. Followers of Christ are responsible not only for the success and defense of their own but for the common good.

CIVIL LAWS ARE RIGHTLY GOVERNED BY REASON

Apart from God's revelation, is there any other standard by which we can measure the merits of human politics? Yes, and it is right reason—that is, the standard of clear, rational thought.

From the very beginning, Christians showed a great capacity for holding their own in the secular world of ideas. For example, St. Justin Martyr (c. 100–165) taught that the Christian faith is not merely compatible with reason but actually enlightens and fulfills it. In his *Dialogue with Trypho*, he recalls his years as a student of philosophy. In particular, he studied the works of the Greek philosopher Plato. The purpose of his studies, he writes, was "to look upon God, for this is the end of Plato's philosophy."[12]

St. Justin presents some of his greatest philosophical apologetics in the political arena, making the case for the correctness of the Christian approach to the common good, and for the liberty of Christians under Roman persecution. In his *First Apology*, he holds political rulers responsible for the wickedness of their politics. He insists that their ignorance of Scripture does not excuse them from the task of governing their people wisely and morally. As he explains,

> [God] made the human race with the power of thought and of choosing the truth and doing right, so that *all men are without excuse before God; for they have been born rational and contemplative.*[13]

Here, Justin affirms the teaching of Aristotle that, since the world is intelligible to the human mind, we need to use our minds to discern right from wrong, to pursue virtue and avoid vice. To confirm this Aristotelian principle, Justin appeals to St. Paul.

> For the wrath of God is revealed from heaven against all ungodliness and wickedness of men who by their wickedness suppress the truth. For what can be known about God is plain to them, because God has shown it to them. Ever since the creation of the world his invisible nature, namely, his eternal power and deity, has been clearly perceived in the things that have been made. So they are without excuse. (Romans 1:18-20)

In other words, since God created us with reason, we cannot renounce our ability to rationally distinguish right from wrong. The implication here is that we are responsible to think rationally, and we will be held accountable for using our gift of reason rightly—particularly in our politics.

As Catholics, we are blessed to have reason enlightened and perfected by our Faith.

CHAPTER FOUR
Natural Law

The Church's teachings on politics are based on natural law. What exactly is "natural law"?

The natural law is the framework built into nature—that is, into reality itself. (This is not to be confused with the "laws of nature" or purely natural processes.) It is authoritative and binding on all human beings. No person and no government can violate the natural law without offending God, the Creator of the moral order.

The natural law can be known by human reason, unaided by divine revelation. This is why it is binding on every human being. God created each of us with the ability to know it intuitively. As St. Paul says in his letter to the Romans, "What the law requires is written on [our] hearts" (Romans 2:15). Thus, those who wantonly break the natural law are "without excuse" (Romans 1:20).

THE NATURAL LAW PRE-DATES REVELATION

The natural law is reflected in the political thought of ancient Greece. Aristotle writes of both natural law and natural justice—and St. Thomas Aquinas cites Aristotle as much as he does the Old and New Testaments. Likewise, the *Catechism* cites Aristotle when it states that "every human community needs an authority to govern it. *The foundation of such authority lies in human nature.* It is necessary for the unity of the state. Its role is to ensure as far as possible the common good of the society" (CCC 1898, emphasis added).

The *Catechism* goes on to note that it is natural law, as determined by reason, that is the basis of sound politics:

> The natural law, *the Creator's very good work*, provides the solid foundation on which man can build the structure of moral rules to guide his choices. It also provides the indispensable moral foundation for building the human community. Finally, it provides the necessary basis for the civil law with which it is connected. (CCC 1959, emphasis added)

The *Catechism* drives home the importance of firmly planting policy making in reason with a quotation from the Roman thinker Marcus Tullius Cicero:

> For there is a true law: right reason. It is in conformity with nature, is diffused among all men, and is immutable and eternal; its orders summon to duty; its prohibitions turn away from offense. ... *To replace it with a contrary law is a sacrilege*; failure to apply even one of its provisions is forbidden; no one can abrogate it entirely. (CCC 1956, emphasis added)

Throughout the centuries, natural law has been the unchanging foundation of the Catholic Church's approach to political issues. By the late Middle Ages, it had also become the framework and standard of Western political thought.

The Magna Carta of 1215 was a uniquely Christian document that, among other things, granted the Church freedom to operate independently from the Crown. The Magna Carta was rooted firmly in natural law thinking and profoundly influenced the development of Western legal thought. It laid the foundation for such essential principles as *habeas corpus*, a rule against the illegitimate imprisonment without legal hearing of individuals by the state. In fact, the natural law forms the foundation of what we now call "human rights."

POSITIVISM: THE ENEMY OF NATURAL LAW

The overarching theory most clearly opposed to natural law in politics is positivism. Positivism is a kind of relativistic legalism that holds that all man-made laws are legitimate as a matter of course. In this view, laws derive their validity from the power of the rulers or governments who enact them, without any reference to a transcendent moral order. In other words, things are good or bad because lawmakers say they are, regardless of whether or not they are morally just.

Much of the twentieth century can be seen as a series of object lessons on the dire consequences of positivism. Fascist and communist regimes regularly enacted laws apart from any moral standard, merely to serve the interests of the state. For example, Nazi Germany passed laws mandating the subjugation—and ultimately the extermination—of the Jews and anyone not deemed "Aryan." The ideology of Nazism called for such actions, which were grievous offenses to the natural law. This was recognized by the Nuremberg war crimes trials, which convicted many surviving Nazi leaders based on their violation of the natural moral law.

Similarly, the communist rulers of the Soviet Union always put positivist policies above the laws of reason and nature. In every instance, the Soviet regime sought to impose arbitrary dictates on the manifest rules of agriculture and production, frequently leading to famine and mass starvation.

THE NEED FOR THE NATURAL LAW

Because it is something all people of good will and sound reason can come to know and understand, the natural law is universally applicable. It gives us a universal method of defending natural rights and a foundation for defending those rights for all people.

The need for the natural law was apparent in the aftermath of the atrocities of World War II, when the 1945 Nuremberg Charter proclaimed certain acts to be "crimes against humanity." The very concept of such crimes implicitly asserts the existence of a universal moral law that is discernible by all men by the light of reason. Similarly, the United Nations established its own Commission on Human Rights in 1946 and produced the Universal Declaration of Human Rights in 1948, adopting policies to guarantee against the use of force in violation of the dignity of the human person.[14] The basis of this was, again, the natural law.

CATHOLICISM IN THE SECULAR WORLD

What does all this have to do with Catholics? Shouldn't we be set apart and disentangled from secular concerns? Actually, no. From its earliest days, the Church has understood that Christians have a responsibility to promote the common good. This means seeking the good of one's neighbors and of society and the world as a whole.

The *Catechism* states that "the good of each individual is necessarily related to the common good," which it urges us to seek together (see CCC 1905). It also emphasizes the fact that authority is morally legitimate only when it acts for the common good and in morally licit ways, according to right reason. In fact, if human laws fail to serve the common good, they can be said to be unjust, having "not so much the nature of law … as of violence" (CCC 1902).

> If rulers were to enact unjust laws or take measures
> contrary to the moral order, such arrangements
> would not be binding in conscience. In such a case,
> "authority breaks down completely and results in
> shameful abuse." (CCC 1903)

Here, natural law finds itself in easy agreement with divine
revelation. As Christians, we know that Jesus, who loved us
by giving his very life for our sins, commanded us to love our
neighbors as ourselves (see Matthew 22:35-40; Mark 12:28-34;
Luke 10:27). So when unjust laws threaten "shameful abuse,"
we are called to be deeply concerned for our neighbors—
concerned enough to have a vested interest, based on love, in
the political efforts to redress abuses and offer relief.

Political efforts such as the Nuremberg and United Nations
charters were promulgated on behalf of our "neighbors"—in
other words, for the common good of humanity. Unfortunately,
these assertions of human rights were high points in a century
otherwise largely defined by positivist abuses. As Christians,
we are called to do whatever we can to further policies and
vote for political leaders who respect the natural law.

CHAPTER FIVE

Patriotism and Christianity

Contrary to popular belief, Christians not only have the *right* to be patriotic; they have an *obligation* to show honor, respect, and affection for their country. Why? Because patriotism contributes to the common good of society. As the *Catechism* explains, the duty of patriotism is based on the natural law: "The political community and public authority are based on human nature and therefore ... belong to an order established by God" (CCC 1920).

OUR OBLIGATION TO CONTRIBUTE TO THE COMMON GOOD

When the Church refers to the "common good," it does not always mean the universal common good of the entire human family. As the *Catechism* notes, "Each human community possesses a common good which permits it to be recognized as such, and it is in the *political community* that its most complete realization is found" (CCC 1910, original emphasis).

In other words, every community, whether it is an entire nation, a particular state or province, or a city, has its own distinct "common good." It is actually on the local level—the level of person-to-person encounters—that the common good is most concretely accomplished and experienced. The *Catechism* points out the obligation of all to work for the common good:

> It is necessary that all participate, each according
> to his position and role, in promoting the common
> good. This obligation is inherent in the dignity of the
> human person.
>
> Participation is achieved first of all by taking
> charge of the areas for which one assumes *personal
> responsibility*: by the care taken for the education
> of his family, by conscientious work, and so forth,
> man participates in the good of others and of society.
> (CCC 1913, original emphasis)

The *Catechism* goes on to unpack our obligation as citizens. "As far as possible citizens should take an active part in *public life*. The manner of this participation may vary from one country or culture to another ... one must pay tribute to those nations whose systems permit the largest possible number of the citizens to take part in public life in a climate of genuine freedom" (CCC 1915). The United States is one such nation. Such nations have become more the norm in modern times than they once were.

THE ROOTS OF CATHOLIC PATRIOTISM

The Catholic embrace of the virtue of patriotism is rooted in the Old Testament. While they were exiled in Babylon, God told his people to promote the prosperity of the land in which they currently dwelled:

> Build houses and live in them; plant gardens and eat
> their produce. ... Seek the welfare of the city where
> I have sent you into exile, and pray to the Lord on its
> behalf, for in its welfare you will find your welfare.
> (Jeremiah 29:5-7).

Later, during the first century, St. Paul similarly encouraged Christians to pray for and honor their rulers in the Roman Empire. Paul recognized what Greek and Roman philosophers had already been teaching for centuries, and what the *Catechism* teaches to this day: The political community is a natural occurrence among human beings. Nations are part of the natural order of things, which Christians believe to be ordained by God, the Creator of that order.

As St. Thomas Aquinas writes, both our parents and our country have "given us birth and nourishment," and "man is debtor chiefly to his parents and his country, after God."[15] Following Aquinas, St. John Paul II teaches that patriotism is a form of the virtue of piety: "Piety in civil life, known in our time as love of one's own country or patriotism," is "a manifestation, with deeds, of Christian love ... [it] is the fulfillment of the fourth commandment, for piety ... includes, as Thomas Aquinas teaches us ... to honor the parents, the ancestors, the homeland."[16] A Catholic, then, who refuses to honor his country is impious; he is acting contrary to the clear teachings of his Faith.

CATHOLIC PATRIOTISM IN AMERICA

The Catholic Church's endorsement of patriotism may seem surprising. This may be because patriotism has been misrepresented as something misguided or even contrary to Christianity in more than a few countries and periods in history, including today.

John Paul II is an excellent guide here. He spoke of counterfeit types of patriotism. An unyielding, narrow-minded "nationalism" is one, embodied by the phrase "My country, right or wrong." It is a sort of "patriotism" that excuses evils done in the name of one's country, which John Paul II denounces as "the antithesis of true patriotism."[17]

Another fraudulent form of patriotism is seeing the American dedication to liberty as an affirmation of radical individualism, amounting to a legal endorsement of licentiousness and immorality. John Paul II saw American patriotism differently:

The Founding Fathers of the United States asserted their claim to freedom and independence on the basis of certain "self-evident" truths about the human person: truths which could be discerned in human nature, built into it by "nature's God." Thus they meant to bring into being, not just an independent territory, but a great experiment in what George Washington called "ordered liberty": an experiment in which men and women would enjoy equality of rights and opportunities in the pursuit of happiness and in service to the common good.[18]

Note that John Paul II ties the pursuit of happiness to the common good. Here, he not only rejects radical individualism but sends the clear message that the American political order must also reject it:

Reading the founding documents of the United States, one has to be impressed by the concept of freedom they enshrine: a freedom designed to enable people to fulfill their duties and responsibilities toward the family and toward the common good of the community. Their authors clearly understood that there could be no true freedom without moral responsibility and accountability, and no happiness without respect and support for the natural units or groupings through which people exist, develop, and seek the higher purposes of life in concert with others.[19]

PATRIOTISM AND SLAVERY

For many today, the historical fact of American slavery puts the virtue of patriotism to the test. Even if it is true that slavery was inherited from America's colonial rulers and was abolished in just eighty years after our founding in 1776, the question of how American Christians can honor a country that enshrined such an evil institution for so long is valid. Here we can look to the early Church for guidance.

In the Church's first few centuries, Christians living in the Roman Empire were fully engaged citizens of their respective states. They were praised for being exceptionally good citizens who "obey the prescribed laws, and at the same time surpass the laws by their lives." How did they do this? One clear example is offered by the author of the letter to Diognetus: "They do not destroy their offspring."[20]

This is a reference to a common practice in the Roman Empire—"exposure." This usually meant leaving a child outside the city walls to die of abandonment or be eaten by wild animals. The exposure of children in the ancient world constituted two evils: First, it was a brutal way for parents to get rid of an unwanted child. Second, babies who did not die were often taken by strangers for various immoral uses.

St. Justin Martyr writes that first-century Christians rejected the practice of exposure, not only for its abortive use, but because "almost all so exposed (not only the girls, but also the males) are brought up to prostitution," as sex slaves.[21]

In the nineteenth century, Christian abolitionists in the United States would similarly work to end American slavery. They did so with explicit references to the American founding documents, particularly the Declaration of Independence, which was rooted in the natural law: "We hold these truths to be self-evident, that all men are created equal, that they are endowed by their Creator with certain inalienable Rights, [and] that among these are Life, Liberty, and the pursuit of Happiness." Slavery existed in the United States *despite* its founding ideals—and it took the bloody Civil War to end it.

The founding of America was not righteous simply because its ideals were codified on paper by men. Like any other human society, it is righteous only inasmuch as its laws and customs reflect the natural law. The rights prescribed by the Declaration of Independence, the Constitution, and the Bill of

Rights already belong to us—they are inherent in our human nature. They are not given or granted by any government, but by our Creator. As John Paul II says,

> Respect for religious conviction played no small part in the birth and early development of the United States. Thus John Dickinson, Chairman of the Committee for the Declaration of Independence, said in 1776: "Our liberties do not come from charters; for these are only the declaration of preexisting rights. They do not depend on parchments or seals; but come from the King of Kings and the Lord of all the earth."[22]

PATRIOTISM AND ABORTION

As we have seen, true patriotism is rooted in natural law. Not surprisingly, false patriotism of every kind tends to devolve into positivism. Remember, positivism holds that actions that we know to be morally evil—like slavery—are made acceptable precisely because they are legally permitted and enforced.

Just as defenders of American slavery sometimes claimed the mantle of patriotism, so too do defenders of a much more pervasive evil today—abortion. To a positivist, the morality of abortion cannot be questioned for the simple reason that abortion is legal.

With the 1973 *Roe vs. Wade* ruling of the US Supreme Court, abortion on demand was imposed on all fifty states. Some argue that this means abortion must be accepted as an established part of the American political order. After all, under the theory of positivism, laws are not based in objective moral order but simply in the will of the lawmakers—or, in this case, the courts. In this line of thought, the reason-based, unchanging tenets of natural law must be excluded from legal decision making. The evil of positivism is fully on display in such thinking, along with every form of "patriotism" that runs along the same lines.

The current practice of abortion on demand in the United States mirrors the Roman practice of exposure in the first century, as well as that of slavery in the United States in the nineteenth century. This again begs the question: How can one be loyal to a country that engages in such institutionalized evil?

We return to John Paul II for the answer:

> The United States of America was founded on the conviction that an inalienable right to life was a self-evident moral truth, fidelity to which was a primary criterion of social justice. The moral history of your country is the story of your people's efforts to widen the circle of inclusion in society, so that all Americans might enjoy the protection of law, participate in the responsibilities of citizenship, and have the opportunity to make a contribution to the common good. Whenever a certain category of people—the unborn or the sick and old—are excluded from that protection, a deadly anarchy subverts the original understanding of justice. The credibility of the United States will depend more and more on its promotion of a genuine culture of life, and on a renewed commitment to building a world in which the weakest and most vulnerable are welcomed and protected.[23]

TRUE PATRIOTISM IS BASED ON THE NATURAL LAW

In conclusion, the Catholic Church teaches that nations, as naturally occurring communities of human persons, are a part of God's created order. We therefore owe our countries love and piety. As Christians, we should seek to participate in public life and bolster the common good of our nation.

As Catholics in America, we have an advantage over many of our ancestors in the Faith: Our country was founded on a robust understanding of the common good as the proper end of our nation and on a commitment to allow full participation toward that end by the nation's citizenry.

In evils such as slavery and abortion, American Catholics are also faced with a reminder of the responsibility we bear as free citizens. As the early Christians of the Roman Empire show us, patriotism can call us to defy national customs or laws that ignore or attack natural law.

Finally, as the Christian abolitionist movement in America shows us, true patriotism and true Catholic witness to the natural law can intersect in a profound way. Why? Because in America, the natural law forms the basis of our nation's founding.

CHAPTER SIX

Power and Corruption

The *Catechism* clearly teaches that there are limits to the legitimate power of the state. The government "does not derive its moral legitimacy from itself. It must not behave in a despotic manner, but must act for the common good as a 'moral force based on freedom and a sense of responsibility'" (CCC 1902).

Laws that are outside the bounds of right reason are "a kind of violence" (CCC 1902). Authority, the Church teaches, is "exercised legitimately *only* when it seeks the common good of the group concerned and if it employs morally licit means to attain it" (CCC 1903, emphasis added).

Finally, as noted earlier, the *Catechism* even absolves Catholics from obeying unjust rulers. "If rulers were to enact unjust laws or take measures contrary to the moral order, *such arrangements would not be binding in conscience*" (CCC 1903, emphasis added).

THE CHRISTIAN DISTRUST OF POLITICAL POWER

The roots of the Church's attitude toward rulers goes all the way back to the book of Genesis. Due to the effects of original sin, no leader, state, or government can be trusted without qualification.

The Catholic understanding of humanity's fallen nature radically affects how we need to look at human affairs. In all our plans, we always have to factor in the human tendency to sin, to make the wrong choice.

As great British Catholic historian and political thinker John Dalberg Acton famously said, "Power tends to corrupt, and absolute power corrupts absolutely." While this phrase has become commonplace among political thinkers, here it is in context:

> I cannot accept your canon that we are to judge Pope and King unlike other men, with a favourable presumption that they did no wrong. If there is any presumption it is the other way *against* holders of power, increasing as the power increases. ... Power tends to corrupt and absolute power corrupts absolutely. Great men are almost always bad men, even when they exercise influence and not authority: still more when you superadd the tendency or the certainty of corruption by authority. There is no worse heresy than that the office sanctifies the holder of it.[24]

What greater occasion of sin for fallen human beings could there be than unaccountable power—power untethered by reason, natural law, or pressure from other centers of power to keep it in check (such as the "separation of powers" doctrine enshrined in the US Constitution)?

Here, Lord Acton simply points out that our tendency to do wrong *increases* when one gains a greater degree of power. With rare exceptions (such as St. Louis IX of France), the truth of this observation has been evident since ancient times. In Exodus, we see how the Pharaoh is overcome with the temptation to enslave the Israelites for his own gain—and then goes so far as to order the deaths of their male children. History is riddled with political tragedies that confirm Lord Acton's adage, including the many atrocities of the twentieth century mentioned previously.

THE CHURCH'S TWIN GUARDS AGAINST CORRUPT POWER

Catholic social teaching takes account of the corruption that tends to come with political power and proposes two principles to keep it in check:

- The principle of *solidarity,* which binds all of humanity together in fraternal charity. To those who would subjugate their fellow human beings, it stands as a reminder of our universal equality before God and of our duty to seek one another's material welfare by the just distribution of goods.

- The principle of *subsidiarity,* which holds that most decisions should be made at the level closest to the people; that is, at the local level. This guards against the tendency of the powerful "at the top" to take charge of all the complex duties and works we owe to one another, starting with our families and our neighbors.

Solidarity

Solidarity means working with others for the good of all. Some might suspect that solidarity would not be an effective tool against corrupt power—rather, that it might actually be an endorsement of state interventionism. After all, murderous dictatorships are known for claiming to take on the task of justly distributing goods, of "seizing the means of production," and dictating all of society's functions on behalf of the needy.

The principle of solidarity, though, stems from two essential truths: (1) Every human being is equal before God, and (2) Jesus came to offer salvation to every individual human person. As followers of Christ, then, we are called to offer charity to all our fellow human beings, regardless of their national, ethnic, or economic background, just as he did in his saving mission.

As the *Catechism* puts it, solidarity is "imposed ... by the equality in the rational nature of all men, whatever nation they belong to ... [it is] sealed by the sacrifice of redemption offered by Jesus Christ on the altar of the Cross to his heavenly Father, on behalf of sinful humanity" (CCC 1939). Practically speaking, solidarity means that we must never deny essential goods to the poor and needy or defraud laborers of their legitimate compensation—principles that are made clear throughout Sacred Scripture.

The principle of solidarity, however, is no radical call for violent workers' uprisings in the style of totalitarian regimes. As the *Catechism* makes clear, solidarity also "presupposes the effort for a more just social order where tensions are better able to be reduced and conflicts more readily settled by negotiation" (CCC 1940). A principle as old as Christianity itself, solidarity must never be confused with modern ideological efforts to gain control of societies by populist appeals to the plight of the poor. The *Catechism* rightly identifies solidarity as "an eminently Christian virtue ... [that] practices the sharing of spiritual goods even more than material ones" (CCC 1948).

The *Catechism* goes on to quote Pope Pius XII's description of those who act in solidarity:

> For two thousand years this sentiment has lived and endured in the soul of the Church, impelling souls then and now to the heroic charity of monastic farmers, liberators of slaves, healers of the sick, and messengers of faith, civilization, and science to all generations and all peoples for the sake of creating the social conditions capable of offering to everyone possible a life worthy of man and of a Christian.[25]

Solidarity must never be taken out of the context in which the Church teaches it. It ceases to be true solidarity—and instead becomes a fraudulent rhetorical tool to bolster ideologies contrary to Christianity—when it is separated from subsidiarity.

Subsidiarity

The *Catechism* describes the principle of subsidiarity this way:

> The teaching of the Church has elaborated the principle
> of *subsidiarity*, according to which "a community of a
> higher order should not interfere in the internal life
> of a community of a lower order, depriving the latter
> of its functions, but rather should support it in case
> of need and help to co-ordinate its activity with the
> activities of the rest of society, always with a view to
> the common good." (CCC 1883, original emphasis)

There is rarely a one-size-fits-all solution that can adequately address the needs of persons. Subsidiarity asserts that problems are best solved by the most local and least centralized competent authority—by personal contact among individuals or by a local or intermediate body.

Some Catholics view the principle of subsidiarity with suspicion, as others view the principle of solidarity. They may see subsidiarity as an excuse to leave the most vulnerable people in society unaided, at the mercy of powerful private interests, on the pretense of protecting them from government interference. Again, were it not for the principle of solidarity acting as a check on subsidiarity, they could be right!

As Pope Benedict XVI put it in his encyclical *Caritas in Veritate*,

> The principle of subsidiarity must remain closely
> linked to the principle of solidarity and vice versa,
> since the former without the latter gives way to
> social privatism, while the latter without the former
> gives way to paternalist social assistance that is
> demeaning to those in need.[26]

The principle of subsidiarity is not based on a lack of concern for vulnerable people who are without advocates in the halls of power. Quite the opposite. It is competent assistance provided by those as close as possible to the persons in need. The

Catechism states, "Neither the state nor any larger society should substitute itself for the initiative and responsibility of individuals and intermediary bodies" (CCC 1894).

Benedict XVI affirms that subsidiarity is "first and foremost a form of *assistance to the human person* via the autonomy of intermediate bodies ... when individuals or groups are unable to accomplish something on their own." It is "always designed to achieve their emancipation, because it fosters freedom and participation through assumption of responsibility."[27]

According to the *Catechism*, human beings are bound to one another not only abstractly, by dint of our shared nature, but concretely, in that we naturally tend to form groups. These natural groupings, made up of individuals seeking a common end, include everything from families to states.

The state is a good thing. It comes from what the *Catechism* calls "socialization," the natural process by which humans always form groups that seek a common good. The *Catechism* warns, however, that "socialization also presents dangers. Excessive intervention by the state can threaten personal freedom and initiative" (CCC 1883).

Therefore, the "principle of subsidiarity is opposed to all forms of collectivism," the *Catechism* insists. "It sets limits for state intervention. It aims at harmonizing the relationships between individuals and societies" (CCC 1885).

Subsidiarity and Reciprocity

An important quality of subsidiarity is *reciprocity*, a recognition that helping those in need is not a one-sided exchange. As Benedict XVI argues,

> Subsidiarity respects personal dignity by recognizing in the person a subject who is *always capable of giving something to others*. By considering *reciprocity* as the heart of what it is to be a human being, subsidiarity

is the most effective antidote against any form of all-encompassing welfare state.[28]

The validity of subsidiarity has been demonstrated in recent years by people who study the effectiveness not only of the welfare state but also of private Christian charities.

In his book *Toxic Charity*, Robert D. Lupton, the founder of several urban ministries for the poor, carefully measures the outcomes of charitable organizations across the United States. His conclusion? Charities that simply give goods to the needy create dependency, perpetuate poverty, and contribute to the formation of impoverished areas of cities and regions.

On the other hand, charities that form constructive, reciprocal relationships with those whom they serve have much better outcomes. By entering into give-and-take contracts with the needy, exchanging needed goods for volunteer work, for example, such charities work toward what Benedict XVI calls the "emancipation" of those in need.

Every human being has inherent dignity. One of the most important ways we honor this dignity is by taking active responsibility for the welfare of our neighbors, especially those closest to us. When governments remove this responsibility from individuals, families, churches, and neighborhoods, they can violate the principle of subsidiarity, making us mere subjects and subordinates in the task of pursuing the common good.

OUR OWN POWER

Jesus tells us that from one to whom much is given, much is expected (see Luke 12:48). He warns us that wealth and security can be a stumbling block on the road to salvation (see Matthew 19:24; Mark 10:25). He also assures us that, with God, however, all things are possible (see Matthew 19:26). The *Catechism* also offers this insightful and encouraging advice to those in positions of power:

> God has not willed to reserve to himself all exercise of
> power. He entrusts to every creature the functions it
> is capable of performing, according to the capacities
> of its own nature. This mode of governance ought
> to be followed in social life. The way God acts in
> governing the world, which bears witness to such
> great regard for human freedom, should inspire the
> wisdom of those who govern human communities.
> They should behave as ministers of divine providence.
> (CCC 1884)

In the end, it all comes back to the natural law. Political leaders
are bound to look out for the common good, as determined by
natural law. The most efficient way to measure a politician's
conduct is by the yardsticks of solidarity and subsidiarity.
Solidarity binds all men to one another in fraternal charity,
standing as a reminder of our universal equality before God and
our duty to one another. Complementary to this, subsidiarity
guards against the tendency of the powerful to arrogate to
themselves the complex duties and works we owe to one another.

CHAPTER SEVEN
Moral Responsibility

As we have seen, *government* is a good and natural thing. Likewise, *politics* is simply the art of pursuing government rightly.

Government, though, does not simply mean state bureaucrats, elected officials, and police forces. Actually, a government should be seen as a nation's entire political order, including everything from its constitution to the moral character and cultural life of its people. Similarly, politics is the work of directing all actions of government toward the common good.

The Catholic approach to politics is radically personal. It seeks to draw you closer to Jesus Christ as well as to your neighbors. The Church teaches that we are called to be a part of our nation's political order ... and, if we fail to pursue that calling, we are responsible for the consequences of our indifference.

A BETRAYAL OF GOD

Catholic theology speaks of the *mysterium iniquitatis*—the "mystery of iniquity." This concept explains the reality of evil in the world, to which the political order is especially susceptible. The mystery of iniquity connects the first disobedience of Adam in the Garden of Eden with the greatest sin of all in the murder of the Son of God. This "greatest sin" of human history was precipitated by a political decision.

In the Gospel of John, Pilate asks the Jewish leaders who handed Jesus over to him why he should not spare him rather than sentence him to death by crucifixion. Pilate chides them, "Shall I crucify your king?" They answer, "We have no king but Caesar" (see John 19:15).

In this statement, the Jewish leaders put nature and God himself beneath the state, leaving no authority above it to guide it and grant it legitimacy. "We have no king but Caesar" spells the end of the Israel of the Old Testament. The very week those words were uttered, as his betrayers conspired to murder him, Jesus declared that the Temple would be destroyed, which it was—by "Caesar" (that is, the Roman empire) nearly forty years later.

The Jewish priests who told Pilate that Caesar was their only king were inheritors of the whole noble tradition of God's relationship with man up to that point. They were responsible for the Law. Jesus, though, *is* God's Law made man; he is the Incarnate Word. He commands us to pursue the common good, to treat "the least of these ... brethren"—those of our neighbors with the least influence over their own condition— as if they are Jesus himself (see Matthew 25:40).

This profound identification between Jesus—the Law, the Incarnate Word—and "the least" among us brings us back to the mystery of iniquity. The political decision to pronounce Caesar our only king was, in a way, the lowest moral point in human history. The mystery of iniquity, then, repeats itself every time we forsake our neighbors in their vulnerability and need.

LEGITIMATE AND ILLEGITIMATE GOVERNMENT

While the Church supports a healthy distrust of state power, it also rejects the notion that government is merely a "necessary evil," as Thomas Paine calls it. The validity of government comes from its place in God's created order, as a naturally occurring grouping of people whose collaboration is necessary for the effective pursuit of the common good. In other words, human government is necessary and legitimate so long as it serves the common good.

When a culture enters a period of decline, however, and its people become unable to govern themselves, they inevitably hand their power over to the state.

As Jesus prophesied, the fall of the Temple and Israel's way of life was already underway at the time of his Passion. When the Jewish leaders shouted, "We have no king but Caesar," they were abdicating their vital role in providing moral leadership to their people; they deferred to the secular ruler of a subjugating power (Rome). Ultimately, this was simply an expression of their culture's degradation. The Temple was destined to be leveled; it was only a matter of time.

As Pope Benedict XVI explains,

> It is not Jesus who destroys the temple; it is left to destruction by the attitude of those who transformed it from being a place for the encounter of all peoples with God. ... The new Temple is formed: Jesus Christ himself, in whom God's love descends upon human beings. He, by his life, is the new and living Temple. ... Thus, the purification of the temple, as the culmination of Jesus' solemn entry into Jerusalem, is at the same time the sign of the impending ruin of the edifice and the promise of the new Temple; a promise of the kingdom of reconciliation and love which, in communion with Christ, is established beyond any boundary.[29]

For Christians, the common good is inextricably linked to the duty of standing with the least among us. The common good cannot be measured by a nation's GDP (gross domestic product) or the Dow Jones Industrial Average. Rather, it is measured by the condition of the most insignificant and needy person in our society.

Because of our love of true and good government, Catholics must stand ready to resist those who seek to govern for purposes other than the common good. As G.K. Chesterton quipped, we should worry about our state too, just as a child worries about a mother given to drink.[30]

"THE THINGS THAT ARE CAESAR'S"

Jesus warned his persecutors about Caesar well before they declared Caesar to be their only king: "Render to Caesar the things that are Caesar's and to God the things that are God's" (Mark 12:17). In the end, his words fell on deaf ears. Not only did they fail to render to God the things that were God's, but they rendered God himself to Caesar!

A great lesson can be learned here. As mentioned, this horrific decision ultimately leads to the destruction of the Temple in AD 70 during the Roman siege of Jerusalem. According to the Jewish historian Josephus, during this siege, the Romans killed armed rebels and unarmed citizens indiscriminately, not sparing women, children, the elderly, or the infirm. Ninety-seven thousand Jews were taken as slaves.[31] Many went on to die in gladiatorial arenas in Rome for the enjoyment of its increasingly corrupt society, while others were sold as sex slaves.

The object lesson here is clear. When we render to Caesar the things that are God's, destruction and oppression by arbitrary human force, stampedes of mob violence, and the general collapse of civilization inevitably follow.

It is of immense importance for us as Christians, then, to consider carefully what we *do* owe Caesar and what we owe God. As Archbishop Charles Chaput writes in his book *Render Unto Caesar*,

> To Caesar we owe respect and prayers for our leaders
> (1 Timothy 2:2); respect for the law; obedience to
> proper authority; and service to the common good.
> It's a rather modest list. And note that *respect* is
> not subservience, or silence, or inaction, or excuse
> making, or acquiescence to grave evil in the public
> life we all share. In fact, ultimately, everything
> important about human life belongs not to Caesar
> but to God: our intellect, our talents, our free will;
> the people we love; the beauty and goodness in
> the world; our soul, our moral integrity, our hope
> for eternal life. These are the things that matter.
> *These* are the things worth struggling to ennoble
> and defend. And none of them came from Tiberius
> [Caesar] or anyone who succeeded him.[32]

Here, the archbishop makes clear that fulfilling our duty to our country is far from simply fending off meddling public officials. Rather, we serve Caesar best by first serving God. After all, our government's legitimacy comes from its place in the God-ordained natural order and from its commitment to the common good. When we, as Christian citizens, take full responsibility for our role in this natural order, we serve the same ends as Caesar and remind him of his proper role.

In that sense, we owe it to Caesar to render to God what is God's. If we fail to do so, abdicating our place as active agents for the common good, Caesar will inevitably become dislodged from his proper place in the order of things as well.

"THE THINGS THAT ARE GOD'S"

When Jesus tells us to render to Caesar what is Caesar's, he is acknowledging that Caesar has rights. Here, though, we need to examine what it means to "have rights." From a Christian perspective, our rights are derived from our obligation to God. We must have these rights to pursue our duty to live well.

As we have seen, a government's rights can be identified by its duty to serve the common good, which is determined by reason and the natural law. Since governance necessarily involves policing authority and the use of force for the protection of citizens, the government has both the right and the duty to exercise those powers. But only for the proper ends.

The same logic applies to us in our duty to look out for the common good as citizens.

RIGHTS DERIVE FROM OBLIGATIONS

Catholic political philosopher Susan Hanssen has written extensively on the understanding of rights that undergirded the American founding. She notes that George Washington had an English translation of Cicero's *De Officis* ("On Duties") in his library at Mount Vernon.

> In the introduction, Cicero made two things clear: Rights derive from duties, and duties derive from some "doctrine of the supreme good." What we call rights, Cicero said, are obligations. And he said this not on his own authority as an inventor of the idea, but based on the ideas of the Greeks: "Absolute duty we may, I presume, call 'right.'"[33]

Hanssen notes that for the American founders, then, "if we have an obligation to do something, derived from some doctrine of the supreme good, then we can claim a 'right' to do it":

> For example, if I have an obligation to care for my aging parents, then I can claim a "right" to care for them. If I have an obligation to educate my children, then I can claim a "right" to educate them. It is my "office," proper to who I am—as child or as parent— and I claim sovereignty over the fulfillment of the rights and duties pertaining to that identity. The definition also acts as a limit on rights claims: If I do not have a moral obligation to trash your property, then I cannot claim a "right" to trash your property.[34]

This gets to the root of what it means to be good. According to Aristotle, Aquinas, and the Church, the man who fulfills his duties is the just, or righteous, man. According to Hanssen, "Only our obliviousness to the historic natural law tradition can make us imagine that 'rights,' including rights to religious liberty, are a modern invention. Justice meant, in the Aristotelian formula, 'to give to each his due.' A just man paid a just price and a just wage. He repaid his debts."[35]

Some debts, though, can never be repaid—our debts to God, parents, and country, for example. According to Hanssen, these are the debts that "the great moral tradition always acknowledged as the highest obligations of justice."[36]

A REPUBLIC NEEDS A RELIGIOUS PEOPLE

This is why religion was seen by our nation's founders as "public virtue." In fact, Hanssen notes, it was *the* public virtue, "underwriting all the public ties that bind."

> It was in the interest of the three great sovereignties—religion, family, nation—to mutually recognize and reinforce the others. Cut one tie and the entire network unravels. The very ligaments of virtue, by which a society runs freely and naturally, would fall limp, leaving naked power—the force of numbers or the force of military might—the only possible mover.[37]

In other words, what Benedict XVI calls the "intermediate bodies" of civil society were factored into our nation's founding as an integral part of the political order. John Adams notes that if the American people become irreligious and impious, the United States would become "the most miserable habitation in the world":

> Because we have no government armed with power capable of contending with human passions unbridled

by morality and religion ... our Constitution was made only for a moral and religious people. It is wholly inadequate to the government of any other.[38]

There is a piece of American folklore that puts a fine point on all of this. Just after the United States Constitution was ratified, a random American passerby asked Benjamin Franklin what kind of government the framers had chartered for us. He famously replied, "A republic, if you can keep it."[39]

As Hanssen writes, a republic is "precisely a regime in which 'the public things'—churches, families, nations—mutually and publicly (i.e., in law) recognize the sovereignty, offices, duties, and rights proper to each."

> When any one ceases to acknowledge the sovereignty and rights of the others, the single imperial Leviathan state has appeared. The test of a republic's health and safety—indeed of its republican legitimacy, of its existence as a republic—is this mutual recognition. If no public agency but the state is recognized as sovereign, then the republic is at an end and an empire takes its place.[40]

Archbishop Chaput agrees, writing,

> A truly secularized United States would be a country without a soul; a nation with a hole in its chest. Such a state could not stand above tribalism in public affairs. It would become a tool of the strongest tribe. American belief in the sanctity of individual rights depends on a God who guarantees those rights, and to whom the state is subordinate and responsible. And this view is not an opinion. It is the historical *fact* that provided the foundation for the rest of our public life.[41]

OUR RESPONSIBILITY FOR THE COMMON GOOD

So what do we owe to Caesar? Chaput writes that we owe Caesar an unwillingness to render to him the things that are God's—that is, our duties to the Eternal Law, our rights as Christians and as citizens. We owe Caesar "our witness not simply as loyal citizens but also as *faithful* ones. ... We serve our democratic institutions best when we love our country; when we nourish its greatest ideals through our own courage, honesty, and active political engagement."[42]

When we abandon the common good for which we bear responsibility along with Caesar, "we're betraying the best gifts we can offer our country: our Catholic identity and witness, and our love," Chaput writes. "We are citizens of heaven first. But just as God so loved the world that he sent his only Son, so the glory and the irony of the Christian life is this: The more truly we love God, the more truly we serve the world."[43]

CHAPTER EIGHT
Prudential Judgment

Just as the American founders insisted on "self-evident" truths and "unalienable" rights, the Church insists that some moral principles are absolute in the world of politics. No Catholic can publicly oppose certain principles without falling outside the parameters of what it is to be a Christian. When it comes to politics, the teachings of the Church do not allow any room for Catholics to promote direct violations of the inherent dignity of the human person.

That said, the Church has no binding teachings about political questions that do not hinge on absolute principles. Rather, it leaves the majority of policy questions up to our sound judgment. These policy questions are matters of "prudential judgment"; that is, it is up to us to apply the moral principles of our Faith when we make these decisions.

CONSCIENCE

The Church teaches that each person has a duty to follow the dictates of his or her conscience. As the *Catechism* teaches,

> Deep within his conscience man discovers a law which he has not laid upon himself but which he must obey. Its voice, ever calling him to love and

to do what is good and to avoid evil, sounds in his heart at the right moment. ... For man has in his heart a law inscribed by God. ... His conscience is man's most secret core and his sanctuary. There he is alone with God whose voice echoes in his depths. (CCC 1776)

Here, the Church references the clear teaching of both the Old and the New Testaments. "I will put my law within them, and I will write it upon their hearts" (Jeremiah 31:33), and "I will put my laws into their minds and write them on their hearts" (Hebrews 8:10).

CONSCIENCE AND THE NATURAL LAW

As we discussed earlier, the natural law is inscribed in every human heart and mind by God. This law is knowable by all human beings, whether or not they have encountered the revealed law of God in Sacred Scripture. This is why natural law is the basis of all the Catholic Church's teachings regarding politics and why it is the measuring rod of all legitimate governance.

While the natural law holds sway over politics, the *Catechism* also teaches that it is deeply personal to each of us and ought to be the basis of every moral decision. So natural law's authority spans the spectrum from politics to personal morality.

CONSCIENCE AND DISCERNMENT

The Church teaches that each of us has a duty to deliberately and carefully "inform" our conscience based on the natural law and the teachings of the Church.

Conscience must be informed and moral judgment enlightened. A well-formed conscience is upright and truthful. It formulates its judgments according to reason, in conformity with the true good willed by the wisdom of the Creator. The education of

> conscience is indispensable for human beings who are subjected to negative influences and tempted by sin to prefer their own judgment and to reject authoritative teachings.
>
> The education of the conscience is a lifelong task. From the earliest years, it awakens the child to the knowledge and practice of the interior law recognized by conscience. Prudent education teaches virtue; it prevents or cures fear, selfishness and pride, resentment arising from guilt, and feelings of complacency, born of human weakness and faults. The education of the conscience guarantees freedom and engenders peace of heart. (CCC 1783-1784)

Conscience, though, has limits when it comes to politics. A well-formed conscience cannot endorse thoroughly unconscionable evils. The Church holds that practices that are fundamental violations of the dignity of the human person and the natural moral law—such as abortion, euthanasia, and sex trafficking—cannot be accepted based on a "judgment of conscience." To accept such objectively immoral practices would demonstrate that a person has an "ill-formed" or "erroneous" conscience.

As the *Catechism* explains, a person might have an "erroneous conscience" due to "ignorance of Christ and his Gospel, bad example given by others, enslavement to one's passions, assertion of a mistaken notion of autonomy of conscience, rejection of the Church's authority and her teaching, [or] lack of conversion and of charity" (CCC 1792).

POLITICAL TOLERATION OF VICE

The Church teaches that certain actions—abortion, fornication, drunkenness, use of illicit drugs, and homosexual acts—are gravely evil. Does the Church, though, require every Catholic to promote legislation against such evils? By extension, should the Church condemn political parties that fail to support laws against them?

The answer has been alluded to previously. Here, prudential judgment comes into play. The free conscience of the individual can inform their political decisions on such questions. But this generous attitude on the part of the Church toward individual Catholics is paralleled in Catholic political thinking more generally.

Catholics who have a deep commitment to the Faith may be surprised to learn that there is a strong strain in the tradition of Catholic thought favoring the legal toleration of personal vices, for reasons explained more fully below. Laws rightly forbid vicious acts that harm others, like murder and theft, but leave growth in virtue to the individual. If Catholics were to claim the right to use political means to enact legislation against every vice, we would forfeit our right to object when others seek to impose laws favoring an incorrect understanding of "vice." Another way to put it is that we would fall into a sort of positivism, whereby we would be granting the state the right to determine what is good and what is evil for everyone, and the authority to force people to violate their conscience. This has been done throughout history. Communist totalitarian regimes believed that what promoted the good of the state was a virtue, which they made mandatory by law, while anything contrary to the good of the state was considered a vice and made illegal.

Political toleration is not merely a historically proven pattern but also a time-honored, traditional Catholic view. St. Thomas Aquinas states that "many things are permissible to men not perfect in virtue, which would be intolerable in a virtuous man."[44] He continues, "Human law is framed for a community of men the majority of whom are not men of perfect virtue."[45] Aquinas agrees with Aristotle that the purpose of human law is to "lead men to virtue." However, he insists that the law must do this "not suddenly, but gradually." Virtue must be freely chosen. It cannot be developed by force.

> Wherefore [the law] does not lay upon the multitude of imperfect men the burdens of those who are already virtuous, viz. that they should abstain from all evil. Otherwise these imperfect [men], being unable to bear such precepts, *would break out into yet greater evils* ... the precepts are despised, and those men, from contempt, *break into evils worse still*.[46]

This does not mean that Catholics should cease to call evil out for what it is or stop trying to persuade people who are committing grave sins to repent. In fact, Aquinas encourages Catholics to keep in mind that even sinful behavior that is legal will, in the long run, be punished by God. He quotes St. Augustine on this point.

> "The law which is framed for the government of states, allows and leaves unpunished many things *that are punished by Divine providence*. Nor, if this law does not attempt to do everything, is this a reason why it should be blamed for what it does." Wherefore, too, human law does not prohibit everything that is forbidden by the natural law.[47]

In other words, Aquinas wisely suggests that we cannot enact laws based simply on what the Church teaches is sinful—that is, by outlawing all sins through the legal authority of the state. But if we do not legislate by the simple standard of morality, then what standard should we follow?

Aquinas replies that the state ought to use the law—and with it the threat of criminal charges and incarceration—only against those vices that are likely to cause harm to others.

> And so human laws do not prohibit all the vices from which virtuous men abstain, but only the more

> grievous ones, from which it is possible for the greater
> part of the community to abstain; and especially those
> which do harm to others, without the prohibition of
> which human society could not be maintained.[48]

PRUDENCE

It goes without saying that Aquinas' argument here should not be construed as an endorsement of personal vice. Aquinas' concern, in keeping with the Catholic teaching on subsidiarity, is that a higher authority (a government) ought not to interfere with the free conscience of the individual. While sinful actions are always harmful, insofar as they wound our relationship with God, some actions cause harm to the life, liberty, or property of others. It is these latter actions that can be criminalized without violating a person's conscience.

As with any other moral action, a Catholic must approach political action in a way that obeys his or her conscience. That includes everything from voting and activism to sharing advocacy materials with friends or choosing a platform and campaign strategies when running for office.

The necessary element that connects our conscience to our actions is the virtue of prudence, "the virtue that disposes practical reason to discern our true good in every circumstance and to choose the right means of achieving it."[49]

> Prudence is "right reason in action," writes St.
> Thomas Aquinas, following Aristotle. ... It is called
> *auriga virtutum* (the charioteer of the virtues); it
> guides the other virtues by setting rule and measure.
> It is prudence that immediately guides the judgment
> of conscience. ... With the help of this virtue we apply
> moral principles to particular cases without error
> and overcome doubts about the good to achieve and
> the evil to avoid. (CCC 1806)

While a properly educated conscience keeps us in mind of what is right in general, prudence is what tells us what to do in particular circumstances. It tells us how to do the right thing, but also how to do it in the right way, in the right place, at the right time, with the right people, and for the right reasons.

In conformity with natural law, your conscience ought to dictate first and foremost that you deal justly with God and your neighbor. As a Christian, you also understand this means you must *love* God and your neighbor. In your everyday decisions, however, including political decisions, there are often many equally valid ways for you to go about that duty. This is where prudence comes in.

CHURCH TEACHING AND PRUDENTIAL JUDGMENT

Let's look at an everyday example of prudence in action.

A friend, Amanda, needs your help. Her car has broken down. As an act of love for your neighbor, you could choose to give Amanda a ride, pay her taxi fare, or ask your sister Jan to pick her up.

Of course, you are free to choose between any of these alternatives. Provided your motive is just and charitable, any of these choices is objectively moral, based on natural law and the teachings of the Church. In other words, each option is an allowable "prudential judgment."

However, maybe you should not give Amanda a ride because doing so will make you late for a lunch meeting. Maybe you should not ask Jan to give her a ride because Jan is a bad driver and might frighten Amanda by driving too fast. Calling Amanda a cab might be the best option.

But one cannot claim that natural law or the teachings of the Church *require* you to call Amanda a cab or that not doing so makes you a "bad Catholic." Why? Because this choice is simply a matter of *prudential judgment.* It is not a morally binding issue.

Moral decisions in politics, of course—such as legalizing prostitution or drug use—come with higher stakes. To look at a historical example, most Americans now agree that it was imprudent to pass an amendment to the Constitution forbidding the production, sale, and consumption of alcohol, thus ushering in Prohibition. In the end, this legal restriction only served to encourage criminal conspiracies, unsavory speakeasies, and the formation of murderous crime syndicates.

Let's imagine it is 1918 during the debate regarding enacting the Eighteenth Amendment. As a Catholic, how can you effectively argue against its adoption? One cannot argue that there is a morally binding Catholic teaching against the consumption of alcohol. There isn't, because the use of alcohol is a matter of prudential judgment. In this case, you believe that the prudential judgment in favor of Prohibition is simply wrong.

If you want to convince people that Prohibition is a bad course of action, you can only do so by arguing reasonably against it. You need to present compelling arguments based on reason and evidence. For instance, you can argue that Prohibition would result in negative consequences, such as the creation of a violent black market, gang-induced deaths, a lower quality of life for Americans who drink moderately, a loss of comradery and trust in communities, and a drop in public confidence in public authority. But what you cannot do is state that the Church forbids the sale and consumption of alcohol, because it does not. This is a matter of prudential judgment, not Church teaching.

From the perspective of history, we know that, despite the noble intentions of the Prohibition movement, the effort was largely an unmitigated disaster. As historian Michael Lerner points out, "On average, 1,000 Americans died every year during

Prohibition from the effects of drinking tainted [black market] liquor ... [and] the corrupt Prohibition agent or local cop undermined public trust in law enforcement for the duration of the era ... [and] the growth of the illegal liquor trade under Prohibition made criminals of millions of Americans."[50]

The Church offers invaluable insights—broad, natural law principles—that can and should be brought to bear on issues such as these. But when it comes to applying those principles to most particular political issues, we are required to use the same means as everyone else to make the case for the common good in keeping with our consciences—reason, rhetoric, evidence, and such. In other words, we must use prudential judgment, making every effort to argue reasonably and convincingly.

There are many policy questions that allow for a variety of options, none of which is definitively commanded or condemned by the Church. In the following chapters, we will examine several of these issues. We will consider which of them are matters of prudential judgment, and which are not. And we will keep in mind the great responsibility Catholics bear—a responsibility to advocate for the common good of our nation, outdoing our neighbors in both love and reason.

PART TWO
ISSUES

CHAPTER NINE
Just War

One of the most revered contributions of Catholic thought is the "just war" doctrine. This teaching is universally respected and used by world leaders and their advisors. The just war theory outlines the relevant factors that responsible parties must weigh before they consider launching any military action.

The *Catechism* begins its explanation of the just war doctrine noting that any just war must begin as a *defense* against an *aggressor*. In paragraph 2309, the *Catechism* then notes the four essential criteria for military action to be just:

- "The damage inflicted by the aggressor ... must be lasting, grave, and certain."
- "All other means of putting an end to [the conflict] must have been shown to be impractical or ineffective."
- The defender must have "serious prospects of success."
- "The use of arms must not produce evils and disorders graver than the evil to be eliminated."

The *Catechism* adds, "The evaluation of these conditions for moral legitimacy belongs to the *prudential judgment* of those who have responsibility for the common good" (CCC 2309, emphasis added).

That's right. Whether or not to launch a military campaign, with all that is at stake in such a question, is a matter of "prudential judgment." But this is not meant to be used as an excuse or a cover for making war. Rather, as the *Catechism* emphasizes, all "citizens and all governments are obliged to work for the avoidance of war" (CCC 2308) and must give "rigorous consideration" to the question of making war, in keeping with the moral law and right reason (see CCC 2309).

THE PROPER MOTIVES FOR WAR

Before examining how the just war doctrine ought to be applied, perhaps we should consider a more basic question: What is war?

According to Catholic tradition, we should first ask, "What is peace?" The Second Vatican Council (Vatican II) offers some insight here. As the conciliar document *Gaudium et Spes* ("Joy and Hope") teaches, "Peace is not merely the absence of war. ... Instead, it is rightly and appropriately called an enterprise of justice. Peace results from that order structured into human society by its divine Founder, and actualized by men as they thirst after ever greater justice."[51]

Peace is a necessary foundation for pursuing the common good. Peace, as we know, is fragile, requiring constant vigilance on the part of state authorities as the needs of the common good shift and change with time. The vigilance of the state is not sufficient, however. Vatican II continues, "A firm determination to respect other men and peoples and their dignity, as well as the studied practice of brotherhood are absolutely necessary for the establishment of peace" as well. "Hence peace is likewise the fruit of love, which goes beyond what justice can provide." The threat of war, being an unavoidable result of our sinful nature, will continue to hang over us "until the return of Christ."[52]

War is sometimes justified. But it is justified only because of the same motives, the same building blocks, that make for peace—namely, a thirst for justice and a love of our fellow men and women. The fathers of Vatican II continue, "As long as the danger of war remains and there is no competent and sufficiently powerful authority at the international level, governments cannot be denied the right to legitimate defense once every means of peaceful settlement has been exhausted."[53]

Nations, then, cannot be denied the right to defend themselves by the use of warfare. Governments have a duty to protect innocents under threat from unjust aggressors and seek to establish justice. This is why we can truly appreciate the heroism of soldiers.

> Those too who devote themselves to the military service of their country should regard themselves as the agents of security and freedom of peoples. As long as they fulfill this role properly, they are making a genuine contribution to the establishment of peace.[54]

The proper motives for war—legitimately conducted to promote justice and peace—sheds a great light on the subject. This is important, because in the absence of these things, war tends to bring with it many atrocities that otherwise could be avoided.

> State authorities and others who share public responsibility have the duty to conduct such grave matters soberly and to protect the welfare of the people entrusted to their care. But it is one thing to undertake military action for the just defense of the people, and something else again to seek the subjugation of other nations. Nor, by the same token, does the mere fact that war has unhappily begun mean that all is fair between the warring parties.[55]

Gaudium et Spes goes on to assert the absolute authority of the moral law during wartime. And issues a historic, unequivocal condemnation of "total war" (which aims "indiscriminately at the destruction of entire cities or extensive areas along with their population"[56]), genocide (which attempts to eradicate whole peoples), and all other forms of warfare that fail to spare noncombatants.

To summarize, war is the use of force sometimes required to make peace possible. The value of this insight cannot be overstated when officials consider military actions. If the purpose of war is peace for the sake of the common good, and if war is to be motivated by the desire for justice and love for our fellow persons, then just keeping this noble view of war in mind can restrain us from many of the atrocities we so often see during wartime.

THE JUST WAR DOCTRINE: OUR RESPONSIBILITY

In many real-world geopolitical situations, some of the four conditions for a just war are met while others are not. According to the *Catechism*, then, war cannot be justified in such cases. For military action to qualify as morally licit, all conditions must be met "at one and the same time" (see CCC 2309).

Again, the question of whether to go to war, allowing that the four conditions have been met, is generally a matter of prudential judgment. Much greater stakes are involved in comparison to the example of Prohibition in the previous chapter. It is because of these stakes that Catholics need to take our duty to weigh the morality of every potential military conflict that comes up for debate very seriously. If we do not, it is possible that no one else will.

CHAPTER TEN

Guns

Guns are one of the most divisive topics in America today—specifically whether individuals have a right to own guns, how far that right extends, and the extent to which governments can restrict that right, assuming it exists.

People on both sides of the debate are passionate about this issue. You might hope that the Church has a definitive policy position to settle this issue. As with most policy questions, however, what the Church offers is not a political platform but rather broad moral principles rooted in the natural law. The Church leaves it up to individual Catholics to apply these principles using the light of reason and our prudential judgment.

One of these principles the Church insists upon is the right to self-defense. An aggressor who seeks to harm innocents can and ought to be stopped, even by the use of lethal force. The tradition of the Church also suggests that Christians ought to submit to the laws and customs of the nations to which they belong, provided those laws and customs are in keeping with the natural law. In the United States, this suggests the acceptance of customs and laws favoring the right to own firearms, given that gun possession is legal (with specific and different restrictions) in every state.

Often, the issue of gun ownership in the United States today is focused on questions about the types of guns that should or should not be lawful for individuals to own. Some commentators assert that today's firearms have little in common with the weapons that existed when the Bill of Rights to the US Constitution was enacted, implying that the Second Amendment does not apply today or that it should be understood in a restrictive sense.

These arguments skew the debate away from its most salient point, mentioned earlier—the right to self-defense.

THE RIGHT TO SELF-DEFENSE

St. Thomas Aquinas writes clearly regarding the use of lethal force in defending oneself—and, by extension, one's family, neighbors, town, and nation—from an aggressor. His views on this topic are cited prominently in the *Catechism*.

> Love toward oneself remains a fundamental principle of morality. Therefore it is legitimate to insist on respect for one's own right to life. Someone who defends his life is not guilty of murder even if he is forced to deal his aggressor a lethal blow:
>
> … Nor is it necessary for salvation that a man omit the act of moderate self-defense to avoid killing the other man, since one is bound to take more care of one's own life than of another's. (CCC 2264-2265)

It may seem odd that, while teaching that individuals have the right to use lethal force in defending themselves against other human beings, the *Catechism* uses words like "love," "respect," and "care." Why is this?

As we have seen, Christians have a duty to seek the common good. The principle of solidarity requires us to treat all human beings as our brothers and sisters, as our equals before God, and the principle of subsidiarity tells us to care especially for those closest to us rather than allow higher authorities to do so for us. Finally, the Church's teaching on just war tells us that the use of deadly force—*even on a massive scale*—can be justified for the purpose of establishing peace and defending innocents under threat.

If war must always be motivated by love and a desire for justice and peace, then similar motives should inform individuals on the use of deadly force in self-defense against an aggressor. As the *Catechism* states,

> Legitimate defense can be *not only a right but a grave duty* for one who is responsible for the lives of others. The defense of the common good requires that an unjust aggressor be rendered unable to cause harm. (CCC 2265, emphasis added)

Here, the *Catechism* is referring to individuals, not governments or military personnel. What the *Catechism* says here about legitimate defense applies even to the use of a lethal weapon in "legitimate defense."

PRUDENTIAL JUDGMENT: A CALL TO REASON

In the current debate over gun laws in the United States, there are two broad positions that fall at least *loosely* within the parameters of Catholic teaching.

The first position holds that the state should make it illegal for private citizens to own firearms—or at the very least, it should make it illegal to own firearms that are especially deadly. According to this position, making all or some guns illegal does not violate the right of individuals to use deadly force for defense because citizens can still flee, or use knives, swords, baseball bats, and fists to stop an aggressor.

The second position holds that the state should not regulate people's ownership of firearms at all—or at least should not make certain guns illegal. This position contends that the right to self-defense is only upheld if citizens are free to own the same kinds of weapons that aggressors are likely to use against them.

In any case, the Church clearly teaches that individuals have a right to use deadly force in self-defense and in the defense of those for whom they are responsible. But the Church has no definitive teaching either for or against the ownership of guns by private citizens. So questions of whether gun ownership should be banned by the state, or to what extent guns should be banned, are matters of prudential judgment.

PATRIOTISM AND THE SECOND AMENDMENT

How does patriotism have anything to do with guns? In the United States, it has everything to do with them. The right of the people to "keep and bear arms" is written into the fabric of our nation's political order, specifically in the Second Amendment to the US Constitution. (The precise meaning of this amendment is hotly debated, and the legal understanding of it has evolved over the course of Supreme Court decisions over the past few decades.)

The right to bear arms was enacted by our nation's founders to ensure a right (defense) that is also affirmed by the Church. In principle, then, gun ownership does not contradict Church teaching. But whether or not this applies to you and your neighbors owning guns is a matter of prudential judgment. This means you must each decide for yourself, using reason and evidence.

THE RIGHT TO DEFENSE WRIT LARGE

There is a strong historical pattern of violence and subjugation when autocratic governments preside over an unarmed populace. As we have seen, the twentieth century was characterized by unprecedented bloodshed, with two world wars and numerous genocides, civil wars, and mass atrocities.

Most of the murders were perpetrated by governments against their own people, whose rights were first stripped away bit by bit as their leaders acquired totalitarian power.

Invariably, one of those rights was that of self-defense. In many cases, peoples targeted for abuse or murder by the state were disarmed long before they were killed. During Hitler's rise to power, for example, he promised to allow "trustworthy" German citizens to own weapons, while at the same time disarming "unreliable" segments of the population, especially Jews.[57]

The United States was one of the few nations spared invasion and atrocities during the twentieth century—though hundreds of thousands of Americans gave their lives overseas in both world wars. Despite its best ideals, America wasn't spared entirely from overstepping the mark during World War II. The internment of Japanese American citizens, an egregious violation of human and civil rights, resembled the actions of our enemies. At the start of that shameful process in February 1942, as anti-Japanese fervor was reaching its peak and many Americans of Japanese descent were already being carted off to the internment camps, the state of Washington disarmed all of its Japanese American citizens.[58]

CHAPTER ELEVEN
Poverty

There are many morally licit policy positions about how best to serve the poor and relieve poverty among our fellow citizens. Catholics of good will may disagree on various policies designed to help the poor and needy. For example, you and I are free to decide whether we favor a $7 minimum wage, a $15 dollar minimum wage, or no minimum wage at all. We are even free to decide whether the federal government needs to provide a "social safety net" at all.

These are matters of prudential judgment. It is incumbent on each of us to make our decision on such matters using reason and evidence. We cannot simply point to a verse in Scripture or a paragraph in the *Catechism* as a definitive endorsement of our particular position.

This is because Scripture and the teachings of the Church simply provide fundamental moral principles. While these principles are objective truth and must be accepted and obeyed by Catholics as a matter of faith, they are not detailed policy prescriptions. The Catholic Church is not a political party but a divine institution whose mission is to sanctify us (i.e., make us holy) through God's grace and guide us to salvation in Christ.

With regard to poverty, here are some of the fundamental
moral principles the Church provides for making prudential
judgments regarding public policy:

- All economic activity must be conducted for the
  sake of the human person, made in the image
  and likeness of God.

- It is immoral to deny our fellow human beings
  the necessities of food, shelter, and clothing.

- In our efforts to aid the poor, we must not commit
  injustices such as theft, which includes the unjust
  appropriation of private property by the state as
  well as unjust forms of taxation.[59]

THE ECONOMY IS FOR HUMAN BEINGS

When it comes to economic issues, the Church wisely
recommends that we never lose sight of a simple truth—all
of these affairs should be conducted for the common good of
human beings. The true state of a nation's economy needs to be
measured by the welfare of its people. As the *Catechism* notes,

> Any system in which social relationships are
> determined entirely by economic factors is contrary
> to the nature of the human person and his acts ...
> [an economy must] provide for the needs of human
> beings ... [and is] ordered first of all to the service of
> persons, of the whole man, and of the entire human
> community. (CCC 2423, 2426)

Thus, the Church rejects any ideology or political philosophy
that treats the good of the economy (i.e., growth, profits, and
power) as an end in itself, without reference to the human
beings whom it is meant to serve.

> A theory that makes profit the exclusive norm
> and ultimate end of economic activity is morally
> unacceptable. The disordered desire for money cannot

> but produce perverse effects. It is one of the causes of the many conflicts which disturb the social order. ... A system "that subordinates the basic rights of individuals and of groups to the collective organization of production" is contrary to human dignity. Every practice that reduces persons to nothing more than a means of profit enslaves man, leads to idolizing money, and contributes to the spread of atheism. "You cannot serve God and mammon." (CCC 2424)

Therefore, the Church rejects any totalitarian ideology that puts the economic good of the state above individual human rights and dignity, such as communism. Such political systems are built on a lie that human beings have no purpose beyond the achievement of material, temporal ends.

This same critique, however, applies to an excessive, ideological capitalism as well. The *Catechism* continues,

> The Church ... has likewise refused to accept, in the practice of "capitalism," individualism and the absolute primacy of the law of the marketplace over human labor.
>
> Regulating the economy solely by centralized planning perverts the basis of social bonds; regulating it solely by the law of the marketplace fails social justice, for "there are many human needs which cannot be satisfied by the market." Reasonable regulation of the marketplace and economic initiatives, in keeping with a just hierarchy of values and a view to the common good, is to be commended. (CCC 2425)

As to how "reasonable regulation" should be pursued, we can turn to the principles of solidarity and subsidiarity, which we outlined earlier when we talked about guarding against corrupt government power.

When the *Catechism* speaks about state regulation of the market, it emphasizes the principle of solidarity, which calls us to ensure that our fellow human beings are treated with dignity as our equals before God. The principle of subsidiarity is also helpful here. Subsidiarity, discussed earlier, holds that when social functions can be performed well locally, they should remain local. It is "opposed to all forms of collectivism" and "sets limits for state intervention. It aims at harmonizing the relationships between individuals and societies" (CCC 1885).

THE VALUE OF WORK

Pope Benedict XVI's observation that *reciprocity*, the capacity of each of us to give something to others, is at the heart of what it means to be human. The *Catechism* clearly has this principle in mind when it insists that "work is a duty" (CCC 2427) and denounces "work poorly done" as "morally illicit" (CCC 2409).

The notion of reciprocity is central to the Church teachings about poverty and work. The fact that the economy exists for human persons frees us from enslavement to purely economic pursuits. But it also places a great responsibility on us, since man is the "author" of work and not only its "beneficiary" (CCC 2428).

> Hence work is a duty: "If any one will not work, let him not eat." Work honors the Creator's gifts and the talents received from him. It can also be redemptive. By enduring the hardship of work in union with Jesus, the carpenter of Nazareth and the one crucified on Calvary, man collaborates in a certain fashion with the Son of God in his redemptive work. He shows himself to be a disciple of Christ by carrying the cross, daily, in the work he is called to accomplish. Work can be a means of sanctification and a way of animating earthly realities with the Spirit of Christ. (CCC 2427)

We are the economy. Rich or poor, we each have a duty to care for the common good. If we are prosperous, we cannot simply leave it to the "economy" to bring about prosperity for others. Conversely, if we are struggling, we cannot "clock out" and leave the hard work of providing for ourselves and our families to others or to the state.

In work, the *Catechism* states, "the person exercises and fulfills in part the potential inscribed in his nature. The primordial value of labor stems from man himself, its author and its beneficiary. Work is for man, not man for work." From that principle, another follows: "Everyone should be able to draw from work the means of providing for his life and that of his family, and of serving the human community" (CCC 2428).

THE FUNDAMENTAL RIGHTS OF THE POOR

This brings us to the moral imperative of the just wage. "A *just wage* is the legitimate fruit of work," the *Catechism* states (CCC 2434, original emphasis). In determining what a just wage might be, the particular circumstances of the person must be considered—his or her needs and contribution to the work being done and the capacity of the business itself.

> Remuneration for work should guarantee man the opportunity to provide a dignified livelihood for himself and his family on the material, social, cultural and spiritual level, taking into account the role and the productivity of each, the state of the business, and the common good. (CCC 2434)

Here the *Catechism* adds, "Agreement between the parties is not sufficient to justify morally the amount to be received in wages" (CCC 2434). This is an important qualification. Given desperate enough circumstances, a person might feel compelled to submit to accepting an unjust wage rather than no wage at all.

THE UNIVERSAL DESTINATION OF GOODS

As Christians, it is our duty to ensure that basic, life-sustaining goods are available to every human being. This is the thinking behind what the Church calls the "universal destination of goods" because "the goods of creation are destined for the entire human race" (CCC 2452).

According to this principle, the necessities of human life cannot be withheld from any human person. The inherent dignity of every person is not earned but given by God in the very act of his or her creation. Respect for the universal destination of goods, however, goes hand in hand with the right to private property.

> In the beginning God entrusted the earth and its resources to the common stewardship of mankind to take care of them, master them by labor, and enjoy their fruits. The goods of creation are destined for the whole human race. However, the earth is divided up among men to assure the security of their lives, endangered by poverty and threatened by violence. The appropriation of property [i.e., the possession of private property] is legitimate for guaranteeing the freedom and dignity of persons and for helping each of them to meet his basic needs and the needs of those in his charge. It should allow for a natural solidarity to develop between men. (CCC 2402)

BASIC NECESSITIES ARE A MATTER OF JUSTICE, NOT CHARITY

Quoting St. John Chrysostom, St. Gregory the Great, and Vatican II, among others, the *Catechism* teaches that we owe all people the necessities of food, shelter, and clothing.

> Not to enable the poor to share in our goods is to steal from them and deprive them of life. The goods we possess are not ours, but theirs. The demands of justice must be satisfied first of all; that which is already due in justice is not to be offered as a gift of charity. When we attend to the needs of those in want, we give them what is theirs, not ours. More than performing works of mercy, we are paying a debt of justice. (CCC 2446)

When we are capable of helping those in need, our assistance is not merely an act of charity or mercy. It is a duty of justice. We *owe* to those in need whatever we are reasonably able to give them. Similarly, St. Thomas Aquinas argues that it would not be sinful for a starving man to steal a loaf of bread. Not only would this "theft" be just, but it also would not be "theft" at all.[60]

> If the need be so manifest and urgent, that it is evident that the present need must be remedied by whatever means be at hand ... then it is lawful for a man to succor his own need by means of another's property, by taking it either openly or secretly: nor is this properly speaking theft or robbery.[61]

This is a truly remarkable aspect of the Catholic Faith! Those in need are due what they need from those who are reasonably able to help them. And if such aid is not given, they have the right to procure it themselves. This in no way contradicts the seventh commandment, "You shall not steal." The *Catechism* explains that this commandment forbids "unjustly taking or keeping the goods of one's neighbor and wronging him in any way with respect to his goods."

> It commands justice and charity in the care of earthly goods and the fruits of men's labor. For the sake of the common good, it requires respect for the universal destination of goods *and* respect for the right to private property. Christian life strives to order this world's goods to God and to fraternal charity. (CCC 2401, emphasis added)

While it is wrong to steal another's property, and it is wrong to refuse to work for what one needs, it is also wrong for those who have property to deny it to those who are in desperate need. The violation of either of these two applications of the seventh commandment leads to social breakdown.

PRIVATE PROPERTY AND THE ROLE OF THE STATE

The Church presents Catholic social teaching in terms of persuasion. It does not seek to dictate the minutiae of public policy. By extension, neither does it call for governments to micromanage social justice in their societies or nations.

As the *Catechism* states,

> The Church makes a moral judgment about economic and social matters, "when the fundamental rights of the person or the salvation of souls requires it" … The Church is concerned with the temporal aspects of the common good because they are ordered to the sovereign Good, our ultimate end. She strives to inspire right attitudes with respect to earthly goods and in socio-economic relationships. (CCC 2420)

Note that the Church aims to *inspire* justice in the socioeconomic relationship between individuals and communities—not to *compel* justice through government-managed economies. When describing the role of the state, the Church projects a moderate series of duties, most concerning the prevention of serious violations of human dignity:

> The *responsibility of the state*. "Economic activity, especially the activity of a market economy, cannot be conducted in an institutional, juridical, or political vacuum. On the contrary, it presupposes sure guarantees of individual freedom and private property, as well as a stable currency and efficient public services. Hence the principal task of the state is to guarantee this security, so that those who work and produce can enjoy the fruits of their labors and thus feel encouraged to work efficiently and honestly. … Another task of the state is that of overseeing and directing the exercise of human rights in the economic sector. However, primary responsibility in this area belongs not to the state but to individuals

and to the various groups and associations which make up society." (CCC 2431, original emphasis)

CARE FOR THE POOR: A PERSONAL RESPONSIBILITY

The *Catechism* contains several paragraphs that directly address the Christian duty to have a "preferential love" for the poor. That is, we are called in a special way to love the poor. It is our tendency to give greater honor and respect to those who are wealthy. We avoid this tendency by making a concerted effort to love the poor first. These passages confront each of us *personally*—and they reiterate the clear words of Jesus himself against those who fail to serve those in need materially and spiritually.

Rarely did Jesus speak as passionately as when he spoke of the abuse and neglect of the poor, whose misery he "willingly took ... upon himself and identified himself with" (CCC 2448). Christians heed these words particularly in the corporal works of mercy, which "consist especially in feeding the hungry, sheltering the homeless, clothing the naked, visiting the sick and imprisoned, and burying the dead" (CCC 2447).

Finally, regarding the public policy and legislation in serving the poor, it should be noted that the Church speaks *unconditionally* about fundamental moral principles involved (e.g., it is unjust to defraud laborers of their pay) but *conditionally* of the application of those principles (e.g., withholding a wage *can*, as CCC 2434 states, "be a grave injustice").

When the *Catechism* uses such language, it is a signal that we are entering the realm of prudential judgment—which requires sincere and careful discernment on our part, based on the fundamental moral principles taught by the Church.

CHAPTER TWELVE

Immigration

Regarding the migration of persons from one country to another, the Church affirms the simultaneous truths that people have a right to immigrate and also that nations can regulate such immigration. Understanding that two principles can come into conflict, the *Catechism* presents each as *conditional* rather than *absolute*—in other words, immigration becomes a matter of prudential judgment.

As with all matters of prudential judgment, debates about immigration are subject to reasoned arguments rather than definitive doctrinal teachings of the Church. Nonetheless, it is helpful to consider recent papal pronouncements regarding immigration and the safeguarding of human rights.

THE *CATECHISM* AND IMMIGRATION

In recent decades, debates about the United States' immigration policy have featured prominently among influential Catholics. It might be surprising, then, how little definitive Church teaching exists on this contentious issue.

The *Catechism* presents a brief discussion of the issue of national borders, taking care to warn us against violating the dignity of migrants but also affirming a nation's right to keep its borders secure in the interests of the common good.

> The more prosperous nations are obliged, to the extent they are able, to welcome the foreigner in search of the security and the means of livelihood which he cannot find in his country of origin. Public authorities should see to it that the natural right is respected that places a guest under the protection of those who receive him.
>
> Political authorities, for the sake of the common good for which they are responsible, may make the exercise of the right to immigrate subject to various juridical conditions, especially with regard to the immigrants' duties toward their country of adoption. Immigrants are obliged to respect with gratitude the material and spiritual heritage of the country that receives them, to obey its laws and to assist in carrying civic burdens. (CCC 2241)

Elsewhere the *Catechism* mentions that access "to employment and to professions must be open to all," including immigrants (see CCC 2433). It also holds that "the political community has a duty ... to ensure," among other things, "the right to private property, to free enterprise, to obtain work and housing, and the right to emigrate" (CCC 2211).

So while there is no official Catholic position on the American border debate, we can take some guidance from our most recent popes, St. John Paul II, Pope Benedict XVI, and Pope Francis.

ST. JOHN PAUL II: WHAT IS A NATION?

In his book *Memory and Identity*, John Paul II writes,

> The term "nation" designates a community based in a given territory and distinguished from other nations by its culture. Catholic social doctrine holds that the family and the nation are both natural societies, not the product of mere convention.[62]

Here, John Paul II affirms the Catholic understanding of what nations are and how they ought to function. Nations are as natural to human beings as families. A nation is primarily a people with a *spiritual heritage* (as opposed to a biological heritage passed down by blood). A nation is not, then, simply a particular land with a certain system of government or a series of laws.

In such an understanding, the nationhood of the United States of America, then, is not found in its Constitution or in its nature as a republic. Rather, as John Paul II writes, a nation is "distinguished from other nations by its culture ... In human history [nations] cannot be replaced by anything else."[63]

Catholic teaching holds that each nation has its own common good, as distinguished from the universal common good of humanity. "Each human community possesses a common good which permits it to be recognized as such," according to the *Catechism* (CCC 1910). This is why John Paul II can say (in 2001) that among our "inalienable rights" is "the right to have one's own country, to live freely in one's own country ... [and to] preserve and develop one's ethnic, cultural and linguistic heritage."[64]

While he acknowledges the right to emigrate, John Paul II also notes that "the exercise of such a right is to be regulated, because practicing it indiscriminately may do harm and be detrimental to the common good of the community that receives the migrant."

In this same address, John Paul II speaks at length about the right of immigrants to maintain their cultural heritage as well. After all, if nations have identities and rights, so do the human families and communities out of which such nations arise.

As we will see, this is also why John Paul II emphasizes that people should not be compelled to migrate due to poverty or persecution in their native lands. The international community must do what it can to promote peace and prosperity in every nation so that people will not feel they need to uproot their families and seek these things in a foreign land.

POPE BENEDICT XVI: THE RIGHT TO MIGRATE VERSUS THE RIGHTS OF MIGRANTS

As Benedict XVI explains in a 2012 speech, "Certainly every state has the right to regulate migration and to enact policies dictated by the general requirements of the common good, albeit always in safeguarding respect for the dignity of each human person."[65] On the other hand, he continues, the "right of persons to migrate ... is numbered among the fundamental human rights, allowing persons to settle wherever they consider best for the realization of their abilities, aspirations and plans." Think of the many people who have come to the United States in search of the civil liberties we are afforded that are not found in many parts of the world.

Through his 2012 address, Benedict expresses a profound love for immigrants and refugees, as well as a deep concern for their well-being. So it might strike us as counterintuitive when, driven by that concern for migrants, he then argues for border regulation: "In the current social and political context, even before the right to migrate, there is need to reaffirm the right not to emigrate, that is, to remain in one's homeland." He continues,

> As Blessed John Paul II stated: "It is a basic human right to live in one's own country. However this right becomes effective only if the factors that urge people to emigrate are constantly kept under control." ... Today in fact we can see that many migrations are the result of economic instability, the lack of essential goods, natural disasters, wars and social unrest.[66]

When the challenging conditions of migrants' native lands drive them to migrate in large, panicked numbers, many end up "living at the margins, frequently exploited and deprived of their fundamental rights, or engaged in forms of behavior harmful to their host society."[67]

Benedict XVI addresses three distinct issues here that are worth pausing to consider—the right of people to remain in their homelands, the dangers of migration, and the controversial problem of bad behavior by immigrants.

The Right Not to Emigrate

Benedict XVI argues that before we assume that refugees and would-be migrants ought to be resettled in new countries, we should consider that many would be better off if their own nations were made hospitable again, enabling them to stay. The world recently witnessed a heartrending example of this phenomenon in the case of Middle Eastern Christians forced to flee as refugees from ISIS.

As Catholic commentator Stephen Herreid reported in 2017, a request for aid for refugees is not the same as a request for resettlement: "Within months of the rise of ISIS, Christian leaders in the Middle East issued a formal statement calling on international powers to take military action against the terrorist threat, and to provide humanitarian aid to refugees displaced by it." That statement "made no mention of refugee resettlement in Western countries."[68]

Herreid continues, noting the need to care for refugees who want to return home:

> Given the amount of rhetoric about refugee resettlement from clerics in the U.S., it's easy to slip into the habit of automatically associating care for refugees with migration. But when Middle Eastern clerics speak of intervening on behalf of refugees, they are much more often advocating for (a) decisive military action against ISIS, and (b) funding and supplies to aid the Middle Eastern churches that care for refugees who wish to return to their homes after the destruction of ISIS.[69]

Dangers to Migrants

Benedict XVI points out the dangers to migrants that can result from the lack of an orderly legal migration system between nations. In his 2012 address, the pope speaks specifically of human trafficking and other crimes against migrants:

> We must not overlook the question of irregular migration, an issue all the more pressing when it takes the form of human trafficking and exploitation, particularly of women and children. These crimes must be clearly condemned and prosecuted, while an orderly migration policy which does not end up in a hermetic sealing of borders, more severe sanctions against irregular migrants and the adoption of measures meant to discourage new entries could at least limit for many migrants the danger of falling prey to such forms of human trafficking.[70]

Dangers to migrants have increased steadily over the past few decades. The last four presidents of the United States have spoken of a growing problem of uncontrolled migration on the southern border of the country. But their rhetoric has included more and more expressions of concern for migrants themselves, even when that rhetoric has also become more heatedly concerned with the interests of American citizens.

As Bill Clinton observed in his 1995 State of the Union address, "It is wrong and ultimately self-defeating for a nation of immigrants to permit the kind of abuse of our immigration laws we have seen in recent years, and we must do more to stop it."[71] In a similar vein, the Bush administration issued a statement in 2007, saying, "We must address the problem of illegal immigration and deliver a system that is secure, productive, orderly, and fair."[72]

In the eyes of the Obama administration, border insecurity was becoming more than just a matter of American interests. Faced with a surge of unaccompanied foreign minors flooding the southern border, the Obama administration in 2014 warned migrants to "not put the lives of children at risk by attempting to illegally cross the southwest border," and it trained Honduran special operations police to apprehend "migrants attempting to illegally emigrate to the United States, often via smuggling organizations." The US-trained unit rescued "at least ninety children" crossing in the hands of "smuggling organizations" during its first two months of operation.[73]

Faced with similar border surges, the Trump administration characterized border insecurity as a "humanitarian crisis."[74] According to a 2017 NBC News report, federal officials found evidence of terrible abuses against migrants attempting to cross into the United States:

> Between Sept. 30, 2015 and Aug. 31, 2016, 508 human-trafficking victims were reported. ... Of those, the majority of victims were female adults of Mexican nationality. Most people taken across the border—49 percent—were trafficked for the purposes of labor trafficking. ... Sex trafficking made up another 46 percent.[75]

"Smugglers use migrant children as human pawns to exploit our laws and gain access to our country," said President Trump in his 2020 State of the Union address:

> Human traffickers and sex traffickers take advantage of the wide-open areas between our ports of entry to smuggle thousands of young girls and women into the United States and to sell them into prostitution and modern-day slavery.[76]

A 2018 *Washington Post* report mentions "cartels clashing over valuable smuggling routes" into the United States:

> Migrants and locals try to avoid being caught in the cartels' crossfire, but the danger does not end there. ... Migrants also turn to smugglers, who often

charge thousands of dollars to get them across the
border. In many cases, the smugglers are tied to *the
very drug cartels whose violence migrants are trying
to avoid by crossing the border*: ... More than 7,200
migrants died crossing the border from Mexico since
1998, or about 1,500 more than the number of U.S.
troops killed in Iraq and Afghanistan combined.[77]

The prudential judgment of lawmakers and those who enforce
the law is absolutely essential here. In his 2012 address,
Benedict XVI calls for the prosecution of crimes against
migrants as well as "programs regulating legal entry, and a
greater openness to considering individual cases calling for
humanitarian protection more than political asylum."[78]

Harmful Behavior of Migrants

As Benedict also observes,

While some migrants attain a satisfactory social
status and a dignified level of life through proper
integration into their new social setting, many others
are living at the margins, frequently exploited and
deprived of their fundamental rights, or engaged in
forms of behavior harmful to their host society.[79]

Here, Benedict XVI touches on the most controversial issue of
all in debates about immigration. As Pope Francis will observe
later, there is no denying that careless talk of wrongdoing among
refugees and migrants can inflame hatred, bigotry, and nativism
against the foreigner whom Scripture commands us to welcome.

Nonetheless, it would not be in keeping with Catholic thought
to dismiss any concerns about the common good of one's
native country, as if it bore no relevance to the question of
immigration. As we have seen, John Paul II identifies the nation
as a community, with territory, distinguished by its culture.
He asserts a right to maintain and defend this culture, this
"spiritual heritage." It cannot be "be replaced."

POPE FRANCIS AND THE HUMANITY OF MIGRANTS

Pope Francis has spoken passionately on behalf of migrants and refugees throughout his papacy. In his exhortation *Evangelii Gaudium* ("The Joy of the Gospel"), he writes, "Migrants present a particular challenge for me, since I am the pastor of a Church without frontiers, a Church which considers herself mother to all. For this reason, I exhort all countries to a generous openness which, rather than fearing the loss of local identity, will prove capable of creating new forms of cultural synthesis."[80]

In *Christus Vivit* ("Christ Is Alive!"), Francis describes the many abuses that migrants endure, both in the process of migration and in the countries that receive them. He highlights the evil of hatred toward foreigners: "In some host countries, migration causes fear and alarm, often fomented and exploited for political ends. This can lead to a xenophobic mentality, as people close in on themselves, and this needs to be addressed decisively."[81]

Francis holds that nations should not fear that migration inevitably poses a threat to their culture and heritage:

> For the communities and societies to which they come, migrants bring an opportunity for enrichment and the integral human development of all. ... In a special way, I urge young people not to play into the hands of those who would set them against other young people, newly arrived in their countries, and who would encourage them to view the latter as a threat, and not possessed of the same inalienable dignity as every other human being.[82]

Francis has also stressed on many occasions the importance of the plight of migrants in relation to other grave moral issues. In particular, he urges that all human beings have the right to life—including migrants, whose lives often come under threat as well.

As he teaches in *Gaudete et Exsultate* ("Rejoice and Be Glad"), "We often hear it said that, with respect to relativism and the flaws of our present world, the situation of migrants, for example, is a lesser issue. Some Catholics consider it a secondary issue compared to the 'grave' bioethical questions."[83] He continues,

> That a politician looking for votes might say such a thing is understandable, but not a Christian, for whom the only proper attitude is to stand in the shoes of those brothers and sisters of ours who risk their lives to offer a future to their children.[84]

Ultimately, Francis' view on migration is that we treat every human person, whatever his background, in a way befitting his dignity as a child of God and to show a "preferential love" (CCC 2448) to those who are currently living under direct threats to that dignity.

A SUMMARY OF CATHOLIC PRINCIPLES ON IMMIGRATION

- The *Catechism* teaches (1) people have a right to migrate, and (2) nations have a right to regulate migration. Real-world applications of these two principles inevitably exist in tension, which renders most questions on the subject prudential.

- John Paul II teaches that nations have a right to preserve their cultural traditions, so a concern for preserving the "spiritual heritage" of a nation can justify some of the "various juridical conditions" which the *Catechism* teaches it may impose on migration.

- Pope Benedict XVI emphasizes the fundamental human right to migrate but urges us to consider the many ways in which imprudent efforts on behalf of migrants can do them harm.

- Pope Francis addresses the migration issue primarily as a matter of human solidarity and the rights of migrants, exhorting us to a preferential love for the foreigner.

In all of this, we should remember the importance of prudence. The opinions of these three popes and the issues of immigration in general should be examined both in light of the Church's teaching and in light of reason and evidence.

CHAPTER THIRTEEN

Racial Justice

Racism is, of course, entirely incompatible with the teachings of Jesus Christ and his Church. No one can legitimately deny any group their full dignity as human persons based on their race or ethnicity.

The *Catechism* tells us, "Created in the image of the one God and equally endowed with rational souls, *all men have the same nature and the same origin*. Redeemed by the sacrifice of Christ, all are called to participate in the same divine beatitude: all therefore enjoy an equal dignity" (CCC 1934, emphasis added).

The *Catechism* expounds on this truth, stating,

> The equality of men rests essentially on their dignity as persons and the rights that flow from it. Every form of social or cultural discrimination in fundamental personal rights on the grounds of sex, race, color, social conditions, language, or religion must be curbed and eradicated as incompatible with God's design. (CCC 1935)

THE CHRISTIAN ETHIC OF EQUALITY

The gospel of Jesus Christ cannot exist alongside racial bigotry. In keeping with the clear dictate of Christ to love our neighbor as ourselves (see Matthew 22:39; Mark 12:31), the early Church brought a revolutionary new dynamic to the relations between various races and ethnicities.

Christianity carried from its Jewish heritage a deep abhorrence of racial segregation and slavery. Our Jewish forefathers had been cruelly singled out as a race subject to slavery and genocidal population control by Egypt's pharaoh, as recounted in the book of Exodus. In fact, the Exodus story gave hope to many enslaved Americans and became the subject matter of many African American spirituals from the slavery era to the civil rights era.

Even more importantly, Jesus' message of salvation is *universal*—that is, it is meant for every individual, regardless of their race or nation. (This is why we are members of the *Catholic* Church, from the Greek word *katholikos*, meaning "universal" or "of the whole"). After their liberation from slavery in Egypt, what set the Jews apart in the eyes of the world was their special relationship with God. In his Sermon on the Mount, our Lord extends the offer of this special relationship to people of every race. St. Paul asserts that, under the rule of Christ, "There is neither Jew nor Greek, there is neither slave nor free, there is neither male nor female; for you are all one in Christ Jesus" (Galatians 3:28).

In a more practical example, as Paul prepares to return Onesimus, a former slave of Philemon's, Paul admonishes Philemon to treat him as "a dear brother" (Philemon 1:16). The implication here is obvious. Would anyone enslave his own dear brother and deny him the right to freedom?

Clearly, the Christian view of the equal dignity of all people is not an abstract biblical principle. Rather, the anti-racist conception of the human person is an *ethic* woven into the very fabric of being a disciple of Christ.

RACISM AS REBELLION AGAINST THE CHRISTIAN ETHIC

Catholic scholar Anthony Esolen provides a thought-provoking illustration of how ancient Christians viewed race.

In a 2014 essay, Esolen writes,

> Does anyone know the color of Saint Augustine's skin? He was born in Africa to a father with a Roman name and a mother with a Punic name. Was his blood Caucasian, Semitic, Berber, Ethiopian, or some combination thereof? No one knows, *because no one thought it worth mentioning.* After the first century, none of the emperors are specifically Roman, and very few are even Italian. *No one cared.*[85]

Esolen goes back a bit further to consider the ancient Greek view of various races and peoples.

> [The Greeks] considered people who were not Greeks to be "barbarians," literally those whose speech sounds like bibble-babble, but their vanity was not based upon race. They thought that people who did not live in a free, self-governing polis were to be pitied; they were missing the blessings of a vibrantly human life.[86]

Cruel condescension and cultural bigotry abound throughout human history. "People will always find ways to distinguish themselves from their 'lesser' brothers," Esolen explains. "But the bizarre racial touchiness that characterized the American South ... is uncommon in human affairs. It is certainly not universal."[87]

Esolen goes on to show not merely the immorality of American racism (for example, under Jim Crow laws in the South, African Americans were often denied fundamental human rights such as food, water, and housing) but also its unmistakably modern character:

> A whole legal and cultural system had to support
> the tottering edifice of a lie: ... that the differences
> between Joe Louis [a black boxer] and Max Baer
> [a white boxer] were more than epidermal or
> physiognomic. Louis and Baer were to be considered
> wholly different kinds of human beings, with different
> kinds of lips and throat and stomach at their water
> fountains. That is nonsense.[88]

This "peculiar" kind of bigotry could only exist *in defiance* of Christian history—which is why the Christian view of the human person was the motivation behind modern history's greatest anti-racist victories. The abolitionist movements in both the United Kingdom and America were inspired by a Christian understanding of the equal dignity of all before God our Creator. In turn, the American civil rights movement of the 1950s and 1960s was rooted in the same teaching and provided one of the greatest examples of Christian witness in American history.

AVOIDING INJUSTICE IN THE FIGHT FOR JUSTICE

The example of a Christian opponent of racial bigotry has become relevant in recent debates about American racism. At the height of the colonial era, a Spanish Catholic priest named Fr. Junipero Serra (1713–1784) intervened on behalf of vulnerable indigenous peoples who were under threat of exploitation by cynical Spanish merchants and statesmen.

Serra lived and worked in California during the period of our nation's founding, at a time when the Anglo-founded Eastern colonies were engaged in the African slave trade and when, in the West, Spanish officials were committing now-infamous offenses against the dignity of native Americans. As the bishops of California note in a 2020 statement,

> The historical truth is that Serra repeatedly pressed
> the Spanish authorities for better treatment of the
> Native American communities. Serra was not simply

a man of his times. In working with Native Americans, he was a man ahead of his times who made great sacrifices to defend and serve the indigenous population and work against an oppression that extends far beyond the mission era.[89]

In 2015, Pope Francis presided over the first-ever Catholic canonization Mass on American soil when he named Junipero Serra a saint. In his homily, the Holy Father said, "Today we remember one of those witnesses who testified to the joy of the Gospel in these lands, Father Junipero Serra. He was the embodiment of 'a Church which goes forth,' a Church which sets out to bring everywhere the reconciling tenderness of God."[90]

Junipero Serra left his native land and its way of life. He was excited about blazing trails, going forth to meet many people, learning and valuing their particular customs and ways of life. He learned how to bring to birth and nurture God's life in the faces of everyone he met; he made them his brothers and sisters. Junipero sought to defend the dignity of the native community, to protect it from those who had mistreated and abused it. Mistreatment and wrongs which today still trouble us, especially because of the hurt which they cause in the lives of many people.[91]

A mere five years after Pope Francis canonized St. Junipero Serra, violent protesters in San Francisco toppled a prominent statue of the saint and covered it in blood-red paint to simulate his murder.[92] Why? They did it in the name of racial justice, because Serra's statue was, in their eyes, a symbol of European colonialism.[93]

The saint's role as an *opponent* of Spanish colonial abuses and as an *advocate* for its victims shows the accusation to be misplaced.

CHRISTIANITY: THE BEST ESCAPE ROUTE FROM RACISM

Secular anti-racism can never serve the same noble purposes as the Christian-inspired abolitionist or civil rights movements. It can never lay the groundwork for lasting change like the work of Martin Luther King Jr., nor should it eclipse the quiet achievements of American saints such as Junipero Serra, Katharine Drexel, Frances Xavier Cabrini, and Rose Philippine Duchesne, who dedicated their lives to the Catholic tradition of racial justice.

The universalization of God's relationship to humanity brought about new possibilities in politics. Most importantly, it led to the conclusion that political authorities could not legitimately exercise their will over people in ways that violate the dignity of a human race of which the Creator of the universe had said, "They shall be my people, and I will be their God" (Jeremiah 32:38).

The law can serve to ensure that citizens are granted equal *opportunities*, but prudence must be employed to guarantee that the law does not unjustly violate the rights of some to provide equal *outcomes* for all. If we have any hope of bringing racial peace to our nation in the twenty-first century, that hope lies not primarily in worldly trends or even in legislation, but in a return to the Prince of Peace, who promises us that his truth will set all of us free.

CHAPTER FOURTEEN
The Environment

The Church's time-honored teachings on man's relationship to the rest of the created world have their roots in the very beginning of the Bible. The story of Creation poetically presents man in an original harmony with all created things, and God's first commands as Adam and Eve set out from Paradise include injunctions to farm and care for nature responsibly.

As the *Catechism* explains, "Scripture presents the work of the Creator symbolically as a succession of six days of divine 'work.'" On the seventh day, God "rests." Here, Scripture indicates "the value and the ordering of the whole of creation to the praise of God" on the sabbath (see CCC 337).

We also see a "hierarchy of creatures" in the six-day Creation, "from the less perfect to the more perfect." This is why we are the "summit of the Creator's work, as the inspired account expresses by clearly distinguishing the creation of man from that of the other creatures" (CCC 343).

It should go without saying that humanity's status at the pinnacle of God's creation does not discount the value of the rest of creation. In fact, the *Catechism* points to the "solidarity among all creatures arising from the fact that all have the same Creator and are all ordered to his glory" (CCC 344). Nonetheless, Jesus tells his disciples not to be anxious, saying, "You are of more value than many sparrows. ... Of how much more value is a man than a sheep!" (CCC 342).

Each created thing "possesses its own particular goodness and perfection," since Scripture tells us God looked on all of creation collectively and "saw that it was good."

> Man must therefore respect the particular goodness of every creature, to avoid any disordered use of things which would be in contempt of the Creator and would bring disastrous consequences for human beings and their environment. (CCC 339)

As the *Catechism* notes, there is an "interdependence of creatures" willed by God, which can be clearly seen in the "spectacle of their countless diversities and inequalities." No created thing is self-sufficient. "Creatures exist only in dependence on each other, to complete each other, in the service of each other" (CCC 340).

Finally, the *Catechism* teaches that "Creation was fashioned with a view to the sabbath and therefore for the worship and adoration of God." Worship, therefore, is "inscribed in the order of creation" (CCC 347). To be in right relation with nature, then, we must respect the "laws inscribed in creation and the relations which derive from the nature of things." This respect is "a principle of wisdom and a foundation for morality" (CCC 354).

ST. JOHN PAUL II AND THE ENVIRONMENT

In the words of the *Catechism*, "Those responsible for business enterprises are responsible to society for the economic and ecological effects of their operations. They have an obligation to consider the good of persons and not only the increase of profits" (CCC 2432).

Here the *Catechism* is citing John Paul II's encyclical *Centesimus Annus* ("The Hundredth Year"), which contains two great insights about the environment: (1) failing to care for the environment can constitute an abuse of future generations, which jeopardizes the integrity of the gospel message in the world; and (2) human beings are a part of the natural environment and must be cared for in much the way we might care for, say, a beautiful species of bird—that is, with attentiveness to our unique needs.

Our proper relationship with nature

John Paul II first addresses ecology in *Centesimus Annus* in connection with the materialistic consumerism that he sees overtaking much of Western culture.

> At the root of the senseless destruction of the natural environment lies an anthropological error, which unfortunately is widespread in our day. Man, who discovers his capacity to transform and in a certain sense create the world through his own work, forgets that this is always based on God's prior and original gift of the things that are. Man thinks that he can make arbitrary use of the earth, subjecting it without restraint to his will, as though it did not have its own requisites and a prior God-given purpose, which man can indeed develop but must not betray.[94]

Instead of assuming his proper role "as a co-operator with God in the work of creation," man himself plays God, using nature without an eye to its inherent, God-ordained purposes. The result, John Paul II warns, is "a rebellion on the part of nature, which is more tyrannized than governed by" us.[95]

If we do not put ourselves and the things of nature in their proper places, how can we maintain the overall moral structure of the Catholic Faith? Will our beliefs not end up being rejected by a world that sees us behaving contrarily to them? As John Paul II states, "In this regard, humanity today must be conscious of its duties and obligations towards future generations."[96]

A human ecology

John Paul II goes on to make a very creative, memorable point that is fully in keeping with the truths of our faith:

> Although people are rightly worried ... about preserving the natural habitats of the various animal species threatened with extinction, because they realize that each of these species makes its particular contribution to the balance of nature in general, too little effort is made to safeguard the moral conditions for an authentic "human ecology."[97]

After all, "[not] only has God given the earth to man, who must use it with respect for the original good purpose for which it was given to him but *man too is God's gift to man*. He must therefore respect the natural and moral structure with which *he* has been endowed."[98]

Human beings cannot be expected to grow healthily and in accordance with our nature if we are denied an environment fit for our species—any more than, say, an animal that is meant to live in a green forest can be expected to live well in a barren desert.

Humanity is "conditioned by the social structure in which he lives, by the education he has received and by his environment," John Paul II argues.

> These elements can either help or hinder his living in accordance with the truth. The decisions which create a human environment can give rise to specific structures of sin which impede the full realization of those who are in any way oppressed by them. To destroy such structures and replace them with more authentic forms of living in community is a task which demands courage and patience.[99]

John Paul II's argument is a brilliant modern reframing of the most important tenet of the natural law, which Aristotle discerned three centuries before the coming of Jesus: Human beings have a "nature," and with that nature come certain inherent functions, duties, rights, and needs that stem from what makes us "special" (a species)—our reason and our will.

The words of John Paul II in *Centesimus Annus*, then, integrate the timeless teachings of the Christian tradition and popular movements to care for the environment. They also are a call to return to a proper reverence for our Creator, as we are the only beings who have been created in his image and likeness—the "summit" of creation and its steward.

POPE FRANCIS ON CARE FOR OUR COMMON HOME

Pope Francis restates John Paul II's teachings in his 2015 encyclical on the environment, *Laudato Si'* ("On Care for Our Common Home"). In it, Francis addresses the plight of the poor, who are denied a "humane ecology," as well as the inhumanity of building cities for no other reasons than consumption and commercialism.

Francis writes, "Nowadays, for example, we are conscious of the disproportionate and unruly growth of many cities, which have become unhealthy to live in, not only because of pollution caused by toxic emissions but also as a result of urban chaos, poor transportation, and visual pollution and noise."

> Many cities are huge, inefficient structures, excessively wasteful of energy and water. Neighborhoods, even those recently built, are congested, chaotic and lacking in sufficient green space. We were not meant to be inundated by cement, asphalt, glass and metal, and deprived of physical contact with nature. ... Frequently, we find beautiful and carefully manicured green spaces in so-called "safer" areas of cities, but not in the more hidden areas where the disposable of society live.[100]

The urgent need for action

In Pope Francis' view, threats related to climate change are now extremely urgent after many years of hesitation. Bold, unified action is needed to curb the degradation of the environment by human activity.

> [Our] common home is falling into serious disrepair. Hope would have us recognize that there is always a way out, that we can always redirect our steps, that we can always do something to solve our problems ... [but] we can see signs that things are now reaching a breaking point, due to the rapid pace of change and degradation; these are evident in large-scale natural disasters as well as social and even financial crises, for the world's problems cannot be analyzed or explained in isolation.[101]

"Because the stakes are so high," Francis argues, "we need institutions empowered to impose penalties for damage inflicted on the environment."[102]

Francis believes that there is "a growing conviction that our planet is a homeland and that humanity is one people living in a common home."[103] This concept comes from an increasingly global interdependence between nations, which "motivates us to ensure that solutions are proposed from a global perspective, and not simply to defend the interests of a few countries."[104]

"Interdependence obliges us to think of one world with a common plan," Francis argues. "A global consensus is essential for confronting the deeper problems, which cannot be resolved by unilateral actions on the part of individual countries."[105]

After all, he continues, "local authorities are not always capable of effective intervention," and so "enforceable international agreements are urgently needed."[106] While individual states "must be respectful of each other's sovereignty," there also must be a more authoritative means of "averting regional disasters which would eventually affect everyone":

> Global regulatory norms are needed to impose obligations and prevent unacceptable actions, for example, when powerful companies or countries dump contaminated waste or offshore polluting industries in other countries.[107]

Francis offers the example of the world's oceans. There are some international agreements against the pollution of oceans, but in Francis' view, a "lack of strict mechanisms of regulation, control and penalization end up undermining these efforts."[108]

Throughout the encyclical, Francis makes a strong connection between environmental issues and poverty. To Francis, they are twin evils, and he writes very harshly against those who, whether by indifference or by ideological objections, stand in the way of tackling them.

He calls for a "more responsible overall approach" to enable the global community to make "radical decisions to reverse the trend of global warming" and to "eliminate poverty." Citing Benedict XVI, he states that we are in "urgent need of a true world political authority."[109]

As things currently stand, Francis argues, the governments of individual countries are too wrapped up in "electoral interests," and are "reluctant to upset the public with measures which could affect the level of consumption or create risks for foreign investment":

> The myopia of power politics delays the inclusion of a far-sighted environmental agenda within the overall agenda of governments. Thus we forget … that we are always more effective when we generate processes rather than holding on to positions of power. True statecraft is manifest when, in difficult times, we uphold high principles and think of the long-term common good. Political powers do not find it easy to assume this duty in the work of nation-building.[110]

Because of the sluggishness and corruption of governments, Francis urges us to exert "public pressure" on them to "bring about decisive political action."

> Society, through non-governmental organizations and intermediate groups, must put pressure on governments to develop more rigorous regulations, procedures and controls. Unless citizens control political power—national, regional and municipal— it will not be possible to control damage to the environment.[111]

The importance of individual and local effort

Finally, short of the global governing authority which Francis argues is necessary, he also acknowledges the role that individuals and communities can play in addressing environmental issues. In his view, the need for such local action is partly due to a regrettable fact: "Whether in the administration of the state, the various levels of civil society, or relationships between individuals themselves, lack of respect for the law is becoming more common."

As a result, climate legislation might be enacted "yet remain a dead letter."[112] In addition, "uniform regulations or technical interventions can lead to overlooking the complexities of local problems which demand the active participation of all members of the community."

> New processes taking shape cannot always fit into frameworks imported from outside; they need to be based *in the local culture itself*. ... There is a need to respect the rights of peoples and cultures, and to appreciate that the development of a social group presupposes an historical process which takes place within a cultural context and demands the constant and active involvement of local people from within their proper culture.[113]

Francis notes that, in some communities, including those of indigenous peoples, a love of the environment is already solidly entrenched in the culture. Thus,

> cooperatives are being developed to exploit renewable sources of energy which ensure local self-sufficiency and even the sale of surplus energy. This simple example shows that, while the existing world order proves powerless to assume its responsibilities, local individuals and groups can make a real difference.
>
> They are able to instill a greater sense of responsibility, a strong sense of community, a readiness to protect others, a spirit of creativity and a deep love for the land. They are also concerned about what they will eventually leave to their children and grandchildren.[114]

But Francis suggests we inculcate in ourselves and our communities the love of the earth that indigenous peoples have "deeply rooted" in their cultures already. And for that purpose, Francis exhorts Christians to become agents of what he calls "ecological education," which aims "at creating an 'ecological citizenship.'"[115] Without a spirit of ecological citizenship, the aggressive regulations Francis calls for will ultimately fall flat.

> The existence of laws and regulations is insufficient in the long run to curb bad conduct, even when effective means of enforcement are present. If the laws are to bring about significant, long-lasting effects, the majority of the members of society must be adequately motivated to accept them, and personally transformed to respond. Only by cultivating sound virtues will people be able to make a selfless ecological commitment. A person who could afford to spend and consume more but regularly uses less heating and wears warmer clothes, shows the kind of convictions and attitudes which help to protect the environment. There is a nobility in the duty to care for creation

> through little daily actions, and it is wonderful how
> education can bring about real changes in lifestyle.[116]

To bring about that change in people, making them docile to
the eventual aim of environmental regulations designed to
curb the climate crisis, we all have a part to play in raising
awareness about the environment, Francis writes, adding
that the institutional Church, too, should participate. "All
Christian communities have an important role to play in
ecological education."[117]

Examples of behavior change

As to the ways in which ecological education ought to change
our behavior, Francis offers several examples.

> [Avoiding] the use of plastic and paper, reducing
> water consumption, separating refuse, cooking only
> what can reasonably be consumed, showing care
> for other living beings, using public transport or
> car-pooling, planting trees, turning off unnecessary
> lights, or any number of other practices. ... Reusing
> something instead of immediately discarding it,
> when done for the right reasons, can be an act of
> love which expresses our own dignity.[118]

While ecological education can be promoted among
individuals, families, schools, and the media, Francis
especially emphasizes the family as the primary place for
ecological education to take root.

> In the family we first learn how to show love and
> respect for life; we are taught the proper use of
> things, order and cleanliness, respect for the local
> ecosystem and care for all creatures. In the family
> we receive an integral education, which enables us to
> grow harmoniously in personal maturity. In the family
> we learn to ask without demanding, to say "thank
> you" as an expression of genuine gratitude for what

we have been given, to control our aggressivity and greed, and to ask forgiveness when we have caused harm. These simple gestures of heartfelt courtesy help to create a culture of shared life and respect for our surroundings.[119]

HUMAN BEINGS AND THE ENVIRONMENT

John Paul II points out that the integrity of Christian morality cannot be maintained if we neglect the duty to care properly for the created world. But he also points out that no true and authentic call to care for the environment is complete without the call *to care for human beings*, who are literally a part of the world's ecology—and not just any part but the most important one.

In *Laudato Si'*, Francis acknowledges that some might be hesitant to accept his bold prescriptions. He notes, "On many concrete questions, the Church has no reason to offer a definitive opinion; she knows that honest debate must be encouraged among experts, while respecting divergent views."[120] There are no "uniform recipes, because each country or region has its own problems and limitations."[121]

As with the Church's teachings on poverty and economics, its catechesis on the environment centers on the human person, on our dignity as creatures made in the image and likeness of God and our equality before him. The proper focus of environmental arguments is the dignity of the human person, who after all is honored in Catholic tradition as the "crown of creation."[122]

When ecological questions become questions of policy and governance, they should be treated as such and submitted to reason and prudential judgment. In particular, *environmental legislation* should be considered in light of the Catholic principles of solidarity and subsidiarity, which guard against the corrupt or illegitimate use of power.

CHAPTER FIFTEEN

Life Issues

Since every human person is endowed with an inalienable dignity, any deliberate killing of an innocent human being is a grave objective evil, forbidden by the fifth commandment.

ABORTION

From the earliest days of the Church, Christians have been outspokenly opposed to abortion, which was practiced throughout the Roman Empire during the first centuries AD. Early Christian writers had plenty of occasions to mention it.

Therefore, the *Catechism* cites St. Barnabas, Tertullian, and the *Didache,* a first-century catechetical document, when it states,

> Since the first century the Church has affirmed the moral evil of every procured abortion. This teaching has not changed and remains unchangeable. Direct abortion, that is to say, abortion willed either as an end or a means, is gravely contrary to the moral law:
>
> "You shall not kill the embryo by abortion and shall not cause the newborn to perish."
>
> "God, the Lord of life, has entrusted to men the noble mission of safeguarding life, and men must carry it out in a manner worthy of themselves. Life must be

protected with the utmost care from the moment of conception: abortion and infanticide are abominable crimes." (CCC 2271)

Elsewhere, the *Catechism* states, "Human life must be respected and protected absolutely from the moment of conception. From the first moment of his existence, a human being must be recognized as having the rights of a person—among which is the inviolable right of every innocent being to life" (CCC 2270).

This is why the Church "attaches the canonical penalty of excommunication" to any formal "cooperation in an abortion," which the *Catechism* calls a "grave offense" and a "crime against human life" (CCC 2272). Anyone who herself procures a "completed abortion," the *Catechism* teaches, "incurs excommunication *latae sententiae* [meaning that the penalty is automatic and immediate] ... by the very commission of the offense" (CCC 2272).

The right to life is based in the natural law and in medical science

The *Catechism* does not present the right to life of every innocent human person as merely a religious precept to be applied only to Christians. Rather, the right to life comes from the natural law and is inherent in the nature of the human person (see CCC 2273).

Hippocrates, a Greek physician and the father of Western medicine, came to the same conclusion as the Church in the fourth century BC. This is why the Hippocratic Oath contains the phrase, "I will not give a woman a pessary to cause an abortion."[123] Rewritten versions of this oath—many of them with the reference to abortion excised—are still used today, and the original text can be found on the National Institutes of Health's website. Interestingly, the oldest hard copy of the oath is housed in the Vatican Library.[124]

It is clear, then, that the deliberate killing of a child in the womb is contrary to the natural moral law—as can be known by reason alone. But we also know from modern embryology that an unborn baby is a human person from the moment of conception—a unique human being, complete with her own DNA.[125] While scientists and philosophers from earlier ages (including some Catholic saints) debated whether an embryo is human at conception or "becomes" human at some point in its gestation, modern medical science has long since settled the debate. The fact that we are human beings from the moment of conception can be denied now only by ideologically driven dishonesty—by lying.

Abortion denies a class of people the right to life

When it comes to abortion, the United States is one of the most legally permissive nations in the world, effectively allowing abortion on demand at any time during a pregnancy. More than sixty-one million abortions have been performed since the procedure was legalized in 1978.[126]

The *Catechism*, quoting *Donum Vitae* ("The Gift of Life"), summarizes the right to life very well in a passage worth presenting here in full:

> The inalienable right to life of every innocent human individual is a *constitutive element of a civil society and its legislation*:
>
> "The inalienable rights of the person must be recognized and respected by civil society and the political authority. These human rights depend neither on single individuals nor on parents; nor do they represent a concession made by society and the state; they belong to human nature and are inherent in the person by virtue of the creative act from which the person took his origin. Among such fundamental rights one should mention in this regard every

human being's right to life and physical integrity
from the moment of conception until death."

"The moment a positive law deprives a category
of human beings of the protection which civil
legislation ought to accord them, the state is
denying the equality of all before the law. When the
state does not place its power at the service of the
rights of each citizen, and in particular of the more
vulnerable, the very foundations of a state based on
law are undermined." (CCC 2273, original emphasis)

In other words, the common good and civilization itself are
bound eventually to collapse once a class of people is denied
the fundamental right to life. In legal abortion, then, we face
an existential threat to civilized society. It is impossible to
overemphasize the urgency of our duty as Christians to work
toward eliminating abortion as an option. Some pregnancies
are difficult, sometimes extremely so, but abortion should be
unthinkable. As Catholics, we have the duty to defend life
from the moment of conception and to support the women
who are facing these difficulties.

EUTHANASIA

Everything we have presented about abortion applies equally
to euthanasia. Fewer disabled and elderly people are killed by
euthanasia than unborn children by abortion. But euthanasia
is the same thing as abortion in kind, if not in proportion.

The *Catechism* teaches that whatever "its motives and means,
direct euthanasia consists in putting an end to the lives of
handicapped, sick, or dying persons. It is morally unacceptable":

An act or omission which, of itself or by intention,
causes death in order to eliminate suffering
constitutes a murder gravely contrary to the dignity
of the human person and to the respect due to the
living God, his Creator. The error of judgment into

> which one can fall in good faith does not change the
> nature of this murderous act, which must always be
> forbidden and excluded. (CCC 2277)

The Church is careful to point out that euthanasia is not to be confused with discontinuing "medical procedures that are burdensome, dangerous, extraordinary, or disproportionate to the expected outcome." Forgoing such procedures is permitted, as a matter of conscience. In such cases, "One does not will to cause death; one's inability to impede it is merely accepted" (CCC 2278).

"Even if death is thought imminent, the ordinary care owed to a sick person cannot be legitimately interrupted," the *Catechism* concludes. "The use of painkillers to alleviate the sufferings of the dying, even at the risk of shortening their days, can be morally in conformity with human dignity if death is not willed as either an end or a means, but only foreseen and tolerated as inevitable" (CCC 2279).

In his encyclical *Evangelium Vitae* ("The Gospel of Life"), St. John Paul II writes insightfully about the motives behind acts of euthanasia: "Even when not motivated by a selfish refusal to be burdened with the life of someone who is suffering, euthanasia must be called a false mercy, and indeed a disturbing 'perversion' of mercy. True 'compassion' leads to sharing another's pain; it does not kill the person whose suffering we cannot bear."[127]

Even in cases where the elderly or gravely ill assent to it or even request it, the Church rejects euthanasia, because in such a case, it is simply a form of suicide, which is the deliberate taking of innocent human life—in this case, one's own.

CAPITAL PUNISHMENT

Traditionally, the Church's position on capital punishment has been that legitimate authorities have the right to impose the death penalty for proportionate crimes. Popes in recent decades, however, have increasingly expressed a desire for the abolition of this practice, especially in wealthy nations capable of incarcerating capital offenders for life.

John Paul II had the *Catechism* amended to urge that capital punishment be abolished, adding to the text that cases where the death penalty might be legitimately used are "very rare, if not practically nonexistent ... [due to] the possibilities which the state has for effectively preventing crime, by rendering one who has committed an offense incapable of doing harm— without definitely taking away from him the possibility of redeeming himself" (CCC 2267).

In 2018, Pope Francis further amplified the matter by having the text of the *Catechism* be amended to state the following:

> Recourse to the death penalty on the part of legitimate authority, following a fair trial, was long considered an appropriate response to the gravity of certain crimes and an acceptable, albeit extreme, means of safeguarding the common good.
>
> Today, however, there is an increasing awareness that the dignity of the person is not lost even after the commission of very serious crimes. In addition, a new understanding has emerged of the significance of penal sanctions imposed by the state. Lastly, more effective systems of detention have been developed, which ensure the due protection of citizens but, at the same time, do not definitively deprive the guilty of the possibility of redemption.
>
> Consequently, the Church teaches, in the light of the Gospel, that "the death penalty is inadmissible because it is an attack on the inviolability and dignity of the person," and she works with determination for its abolition worldwide. (CCC 2267)[128]

The preceding paragraph of the *Catechism*, which has not been changed, presents the overall tradition of Catholic thought on the death penalty, noting,

> Legitimate public authority has the right and duty to inflict punishment proportionate to the gravity of the offense. Punishment has the primary aim of redressing the disorder introduced by the offense. (CCC 2266)

Later in the same paragraph, the *Catechism* passingly mentions that "punishment" serves two functions: "defending public order and protecting people's safety."

Both John Paul II and Francis frame capital punishment, though, exclusively in terms of defending the public from the physical threat of the criminal in question. In this, some have seen a contradiction between the long-standing Catholic teaching that the death penalty is a "right and duty [of legitimate authority] to inflict punishment proportionate to the gravity of the offense" (CCC 2266) and the more recent statements of popes that frame it as "inadmissible" and "an attack on the inviolability and dignity of the person" (CCC 2267).

In 2004, as prefect of the Vatican's Congregation for the Doctrine of the Faith, Pope Benedict XVI (then Cardinal Joseph Ratzinger) took a similar view of John Paul II's revision of the *Catechism's* death penalty. That is, Cardinal Ratzinger viewed it as "prudential guidance" rather than as a binding and definitive teaching of the Church.

As Cardinal Ratzinger writes,

> Not all moral issues have the same moral weight as abortion and euthanasia. For example, if a Catholic were to be at odds with the Holy Father on the application of capital punishment ... he would not for that reason be considered unworthy to present himself to receive Holy Communion. While the Church exhorts civil authorities ... to exercise discretion and mercy in imposing punishment on criminals, it may still be permissible ... to have recourse to capital punishment. There may be a legitimate diversity of opinion even among Catholics about ... applying the death penalty, but not however with regard to abortion and euthanasia.[129]

If Ratzinger could hold this view of John Paul II's teaching on the death penalty, it would seem applicable to Francis' position as well. So while a Catholic can hold that *in principle* capital punishment is permissible, recent statements of the popes raise the bar significantly in terms of its legitimate use.

WHEN PRUDENTIAL JUDGMENT FLIRTS WITH DEATH

As we have seen, the Church distinguishes between absolute, inviolable moral imperatives and prudential conclusions. Catholics are not free to reject the Church's absolute moral principles without falling into serious sin. This is an important distinction to keep in mind when politicians reject an absolute moral position of the Church but hold the same prudential positions as you on any number of other issues.

For example, imagine if a politician holds, as you do, the following positions: (1) Catholic parochial schools should be publicly supported through tax-funded school vouchers for families, and (2) there should be a tax relief program for those who pay off their student debt within ten years of graduation. These are all prudential policy positions that you agree with.

But he also believes that the United States should fund Marie Stopes International, an advocacy-medical group that lobbies for the legalization of abortion in African countries like Nigeria. As much as you agree with him on the prudential questions, you cannot support him. Abortion is not a prudential question; it is an absolute moral issue.

As Cardinal Ratzinger states,

> The Church teaches that abortion or euthanasia is a grave sin. The Encyclical Letter *Evangelium vitae*, with reference to judicial decisions or civil laws that authorize or promote abortion or euthanasia, states that there is a "grave and clear obligation to oppose them by conscientious objection. [...] In the case of

> an intrinsically unjust law, such as a law permitting
> abortion or euthanasia, it is therefore never licit to
> obey it, or to 'take part in a propaganda campaign in
> favor of such a law or vote for it'" [EV 73]. Christians
> have a "grave obligation of conscience not to cooperate
> formally in practices which, even if permitted by civil
> legislation, are contrary to God's law. Indeed, from the
> moral standpoint, it is never licit to cooperate formally
> in evil. [...] This cooperation can never be justified
> either by invoking respect for the freedom of others
> or by appealing to the fact that civil law permits it or
> requires it."[130]

But what if undocumented migrants are being desperately underpaid? What if a proposed environmental regulation facilitates businesses dumping fatally toxic waste near homes of vulnerable families? There are any number of ways that the fundamental dignity of human beings can be threatened to a degree that ought to keep us, as Catholics, from supporting a given politician or policy.

Prudential judgment can never legitimately conclude that patent violations of the moral law are permissible. As Christians, we understand that abortion is always and everywhere gravely wrong. Euthanasia is always and everywhere gravely wrong.

Denying the right to life is not simply a gravely evil act on the part of the doctor who performs an abortion or the family member who assists in his sick relative's suicide. It is an act that calls into question the legitimacy of any government that allows it, and it undermines "the very foundations of a state" (CCC 2273).

CHAPTER SIXTEEN

Human Sexuality, Marriage, and Family

Ultimately, the Catholic understanding of human sexuality is concerned with the happiness and fulfillment of every human person. It would not be an exaggeration to say the Church teaches that the fate of nations depends on human sexuality having its proper place in society.

HUMAN SEXUALITY AND FAMILY

For Catholics, human sexuality has a purpose, just like every other human faculty.

Our intellect, for instance, has the purpose of discerning the truth. Our will has the purpose of choosing to act according to the truths our minds discern. Our sexuality has the purpose of bonding a man and a woman together in marriage for the creation of a family.

The family has a vital, reciprocal relationship with the political community. It is two things at once:

- The family is the most personal, intimate, and formative place for the individual human person. A healthy political community protects and honors the family at all costs.

- The family is also the most important institution for the public good of all persons. No political community can survive without healthy families supporting it.

The *Catechism's* passages on the family constantly intermingle these two points. The family is the *"original cell of social life,"* the *Catechism* states (CCC 2207). "It is the natural society" out of which all higher social groups emerge and for the sake of which those higher groups ought to exist.

"Authority, stability, and a life of relationships within the family constitute the foundations for freedom, security, and fraternity within society," the *Catechism* continues. "The family is the community in which, from childhood, one can learn moral values, begin to honor God, and make good use of freedom" (CCC 2207).

After all, by nature we are not individuals born directly into the public. We are born into families and enter public life by way of them. That's why the fourth commandment ("Honor your father and your mother") "extends to the duties of pupils to teachers, employees to employers, subordinates to leaders, citizens to their country, and to those who administer or govern it," according to the *Catechism*, and that commandment "includes and presupposes the duties" not only of parents but also of "instructors, teachers, leaders, magistrates, those who govern, all who exercise authority over others or over a community of persons" (CCC 2199).

This is why the future of our nation—and any nation—depends on the family. "Family life is an initiation into life in society" (CCC 2207). If the initiation goes wrong, or worse, there is no initiation at all due to a total loss of family structure, then we will be reduced to a loose, volatile collection of wandering individuals with no basis to relate to one another or to seek an agreed common good.

Marriage and family are the *proper ends* of human sexuality. What does it mean for marriage and family to be the "proper ends" of human sexuality? Isn't sex a private matter? Does it really have so much to do with public policy or politics? To answer these questions, let us briefly examine Catholic anthropology as it relates to politics.

THE HUMAN PERSON AND POLITICS

Catholic political thought is based in nature. Specifically, the *nature of the human person* provides the foundation for virtually all of the Church's political tenets.

As we have seen, Aristotle teaches that human beings have a specific nature, meaning that we have been designed with certain functions, rights, and duties. When we come to understand our nature and live according to it, this is called virtue—which is the only path to human happiness.

Catholics agree with Aristotle. But we put things a little differently.

A knowable, personal God gave us our nature. When God created us, he wrote an eternal law "on our hearts"—a sort of instruction manual for virtue (which is how Aristotle himself got as far as he did in discerning the truth of our nature). And finally, if we live virtuously, we are indeed on the path to happiness. This happiness, ultimately, is being united with our Creator in eternity— heaven. (The alternate path, living contrary to our nature, is sin and leads to unhappiness. Ultimately, it leads to our eternal separation from our Creator, in hell.)

When we accept our true nature and strive to live according to it, we embrace ourselves as God created us to be. By accepting his good work in us, we embrace God himself. When we reject our nature, we reject the way God created us, and, ultimately, we reject him.

The purpose of politics, according to both Aristotle and the Church, is to create and maintain a just order in a people and nation. Why? Because a just nation is needed to facilitate virtue and happiness in its citizens.

As the founders of the United States understood, granting freedom to its people is necessary to allow for the pursuit of virtue and happiness. But what is freedom? The *Catechism* states,

> Freedom is the power, rooted in reason and will, to act or not to act, to do this or that, and so to perform deliberate actions on one's own responsibility. By free will one shapes one's own life. Human freedom is a force for growth and maturity in truth and goodness; it attains its perfection when directed toward God, our beatitude. (CCC 1731)

In addition, "Every human person … has the natural right to be recognized as a free and responsible being" (CCC 1738).

> All owe to each other this duty of respect. The *right to the exercise of freedom*, especially in moral and religious matters, is an inalienable requirement of the dignity of the human person. This right must be recognized and protected by civil authority within the limits of the common good and public order. (CCC 1738, original emphasis)

If a nation denies its citizens the right to choose between good and bad, it is not facilitating their virtue and happiness but preventing them from truly pursuing it—an endeavor that requires the exercise of their free will.

That said, the purpose of freedom is the pursuit of happiness by way of virtue. So for a state to promote or encourage vice would also be a failure. "The more one does what is good, the freer one becomes," the *Catechism* teaches. "There is no true freedom except in the service of what is good and just. The choice to disobey and do evil is an abuse of freedom and leads to 'the slavery of sin'" (CCC 1733).

DISORDERED SEXUALITY

As we have seen, the Church teaches that human sexual acts must be expressed within marriage, as intended by their nature. Marriage has a two-fold purpose: (1) the joining of a man and a woman in marriage for their mutual good, and (2) the procreation of children. Sexual activity outside of marriage is sinful because it is against the intended use for which God created it and gave it to us. Sexuality apart from marriage is *disordered*.

Nations should seek to facilitate the proper role of sexuality within marriage, because the family is the primary "cell" of society from which all higher groupings and institutions are formed and maintained. Given our current political climate, however, this is a difficult position for many politicians—and even faithful Catholics—to promote.

For example, the Church acknowledges that homosexual acts are "intrinsically disordered" (CCC 2357)—that is, such acts are contrary to our purpose as men and women created in God's image and likeness and our call to free, total, faithful, and fruitful marital love. Still, the Church maintains that those whose sexual impulses attract them exclusively or predominantly to members of the same sex "must be accepted with respect, compassion, and sensitivity. Every sign of unjust discrimination in their regard should be avoided. These persons are called to fulfill God's will in their lives" (CCC 2358).

Tragically, the 2015 legalization of "same-sex marriage" by the US Supreme Court has been used as a vehicle for direct attacks on the role of marriage and family in society. It is difficult for Christians to speak out against this new reality or defend the Christian view of marriage without being mocked or ostracized. Unfortunately, same-sex attraction is now broadly viewed as an "identity" associated with a political ideology rather than simply one of mankind's many struggles that tempt him to reject his own nature and the path to virtue and happiness it offers.

Similarly, the "transgender" political movement advocates acts that are perhaps the most blatant rejections of human nature short of murder or suicide—the physical removal and surgical replacement of a person's sexual organs. The *Catechism* addresses such actions in the same segment in which it addresses terrorism and torture: "Except when performed for strictly therapeutic medical reasons, directly intended *amputations*, *mutilations*, and *sterilizations* performed on innocent persons are against the moral law" (CCC 2297, original emphasis).

THE GREAT GIFT OF CHRISTIAN TEACHINGS ON SEXUALITY

Since the so-called "sexual revolution" of the 1960s, a growing segment in our society has decried the Christian understanding of human sexuality as backwards, repressive, and even cruel. Few realize that it is the Church's attitude toward sex that got us to where we are today.

Since the first century, Christian leaders have preached the dignity of all human persons, no matter how low their social status. In the Church, young women (and even men) found the confidence they needed to reject the rude sexual advances of powerful men. Many died rather than let themselves be sexually degraded. At long last, their witness to the Christian embrace of human sexuality would be honored with a place in the laws of modern nations.

Even historian Tom Holland, an avowed atheist, recognizes the great contribution Christian thought has made when it comes to sex. Jonathon van Maren summarizes Holland's thinking:

> While studying the ancient world, Holland ... realized something. Simply, the ancients were cruel, and their values utterly foreign to him. ... The bodies

> of slaves were treated like outlets for the physical pleasure of those with power. ... The poor and the weak had no rights.
>
> How did we get from there to here? It was Christianity, Holland writes. Christianity revolutionized sex and marriage, demanding that men control themselves and prohibiting all forms of rape. Christianity confined sexuality within monogamy. (It is ironic, Holland notes, that these are now the very standards for which Christianity is derided.) Christianity elevated women. In short, Christianity utterly transformed the world.[131]

How did the Christian understanding of sex accomplish this transformation of the world? Simply by being respectful of the reality of the human person as he or she is created, rather than rejecting our nature as if we were not good enough or as if our God had created us poorly.

This certainly is good news because each of us is naturally a child of a man and a woman. By insisting on the true nature of human sexuality, the Church safeguards what most of us intuitively know to be ideal (which, incidentally, even secular psychology confirms)—a loving home, the knowledge of who our mother and father are, and a childhood full of first-hand quality time with them both.

Beyond the historical merits of these teachings, and beyond even the practical benefits of intact homelifes for ourselves and for society more broadly, there is a more profound value to accepting our true sexuality.

Buried among the *Catechism's* paragraphs on the subject of sex is a quotation from St. John Chrysostom in the fourth century:

> St. John Chrysostom suggests that young husbands should say to their wives: I have taken you in my arms, and I love you, and I prefer you to my life itself.

> For the present life is nothing, and my most ardent
> dream is to spend it with you in such a way that we
> may be assured of not being separated in the life
> reserved for us. ... I place your love above all things,
> and nothing would be more bitter or painful to me
> than to be of a different mind than you. (CCC 2365)

The words Chrysostom recommends between lovers express exactly what should exist between each of us and the truths inherent in reality—including the truth of our sexuality.

All of us, and perhaps especially those of us who are single, sexually confused, homosexually inclined, or gender dysphoric, should approach the way God created us—should approach ourselves—with this loving and accepting attitude. And we should live in full confidence that God is the source of all goodness, all joy, and it is ultimately through our relationship with him that we will experience the fulfillment of our deepest desires.

Regardless of your background, you can say to the loving God who created you as you are, and to the eternal truths about yourself as a human person: "I love you. ... Nothing would be more bitter or painful to me than to be of a different mind than you."

EPILOGUE

Religious Liberty for the Sake of All

Religious liberty, the free exercise of religion, is a necessity without which we cannot effectively do our duty to God and neighbor. All of the treasures of Catholic wisdom pertaining to public life are meant not only for us, but for the world. In choosing to follow Christ, we choose to obey the God-man who commands us to change the world, and the lives of our neighbors, for the better.

Liberty is the key that unlocks the door to that great adventure.

In its passages on religious liberty, the *Catechism* teaches us that all men "are bound to seek the truth, especially in what concerns God and his Church, and to embrace it and hold on to it as they come to know it" (CCC 2104).

This is what we have sought to do—to assist in that search— throughout the chapters of this book.

Since *all* men are called to that effort, and not just us, it doesn't "contradict a 'sincere respect' for different religions which frequently 'reflect a ray of that truth which enlightens all men'" (CCC 2104).

"By constantly evangelizing men," we are meant to enable them "to infuse the Christian spirit into the mentality and mores, laws and structures of the communities" in which we reside, whether or not we live to see them formally enter the Church:

> The social duty of Christians is to respect and awaken in each man the love of the true and the good. It requires them to make known the worship of the one true religion which subsists in the Catholic and apostolic Church. Christians are called to be the light of the world. Thus, the Church shows forth the kingship of Christ over all creation and in particular over human societies. (CCC 2105)

Religious liberty, though, is not about gaining a prominent place in society for Catholics. Rather, it is about changing the world to reflect the truth, the order of things as they were created to be, infused with the happiness that is only achieved when creatures come face to face with what they are made for—glory.

Religious liberty represents the universal call of God to human beings. He calls out to all people—calls them to himself. As Christians, we have the great mission of answering that call by echoing it to all around us who may have grown deaf to it because of humankind's fallen, sinful nature. We are meant to bring to our world the generosity, the providence, the love-unto-death that Our Lord offers to all mankind.

As we read in the letter to Diognetus, God sent his Son as a messenger, not as a despot:

> Was it then, as one might conceive, for the purpose of exercising tyranny, or of inspiring fear and terror? By no means, but under the influence of clemency and meekness. As a king sends his son, who is also a king, so sent He Him; as God He sent Him; as to men He sent Him; as a Savior He sent Him, and as seeking to persuade, not to compel us.[132]

We are meant to approach our neighbors with a similar attitude. "Nobody may be forced to act against his convictions," the *Catechism* tells us, "nor is anyone to be restrained from acting in accordance with his conscience in religious matters in private or in public, alone or in association with others, within due limits":

> This right [to religious liberty] is based on the very nature of the human person, whose dignity enables him freely to assent to the divine truth which transcends the temporal order. For this reason it "continues to exist even in those who do not live up to their obligation of seeking the truth and adhering to it." (CCC 2106)

In other words, advocating for our own liberty as Catholics is incompatible with a desire for the suppression of others' liberty. Their right to seek the truth and, in conscience, follow it isn't based on whether they are Christian but on the fact that they are human—a fact which we as Christians are forbidden to question.

Finally, this universal acceptance of the humanity of our neighbors forms the basis of virtually all the moral tenets we must bring to bear in public life.

Voting is a vital way in which we participate in public life. It is one of our fundamental political rights (and obligations), hard-won by the generations that came before us.

FOR THE SAKE OF OTHERS, WE MUST BE FREE

Think about it. It is Christians more than anyone else who hold the moral truths that make civilization flourish. Even practically speaking, it was overwhelmingly Christians and those they managed to persuade who led the successful effort to abolish American slavery. Today, it is Christians who lead the way in advocating for the unborn child.

Now imagine if Christians were suddenly removed from the public equation because of the suppression of our religious freedom. Who then would speak for the oppressed and the abandoned?

Christ made us responsible for the common good, and especially for the least of our brethren, who live under the most clear and present threats to their dignity. It is by acting on that responsibility publicly that we gather allies in the service and defense of our fellow men—whether or not those allies join us immediately in the communion of the Catholic Faith.

That is why it is not an option for Christians to give up religious liberty. It is not some possession of ours which we can discard at will, and it would not be a simple, private act of self-denial to exchange our religious freedom for oppression.

On the other hand, we do not owe our religious liberty to ourselves, nor any of the riches of our faith. We owe it all to God, and to the neighbors he sent us to serve.

Notes

1. Aristotle, *Politics* 1.2.

2. Aristotle, *Nicomachean Ethics* 10.8.

3. Russell Kirk, *The Roots of American Order* (LaSalle, IL: Open Court, 1977), 90.

4. Kirk, 197-198.

5. "A Traditional Catechetical Formula," in CCC Part Two, Section Three: The Ten Commandments.

6. Epistle to Diognetus (Mathetes), chapter 5.

7. Joseph Ratzinger (Pope Benedict XVI), *Jesus of Nazareth*, part 1, *From the Baptism in the Jordan to the Transfiguration*, trans. Adrian J. Walker (New York: Doubleday, 2007), 114-115.

8 Ratzinger, 116.

9. Ratzinger.

10. Diognetus, chapter 5.

11. Ratzinger, *Jesus of Nazareth*, 118.

12. Justin Martyr, *Dialogue with Trypho,* chapter 2.

13. Justin Martyr, *The First Apology*, chapter 28 (emphasis added).

14. "Universal Declaration of Human Rights," United Nations, December 10, 1948, available at un.org/.

15.   Thomas Aquinas, *Summa Theologica* II–II.101.1.

16.   John Paul II, Homily at Benjamín Matienzo Airport (Tucumán, Argentina), April 8, 1987.

17.   John Paul II, United Nations Headquarters (New York), October 5, 1995.

18.   John Paul II, Address to H.E. Mrs. Corine (Lindy) Claiborne Boggs, new ambassador of the United States of America to the Holy See (December 16, 1997), vatican.va/.

19.   John Paul II.

20.   Diognetus, chapter 5.

21.   Justin Martyr, *First Apology*, 27.

22.   John Paul II, Address to Boggs.

23.   John Paul II.

24.   John Emerich Edward Dalberg Acton, "Letter I, Acton-Creighton Correspondence," in *Lectures on Modern History*, ed. Reginald Vere Laurence and John Neville Figgis (London: Macmillan, 1906).

25.   CCC 1942, citing Pius XII, Discourse (June 1, 1941).

26.   Benedict XVI, *Caritas in Veritate* 58.

27.   Benedict XVI, 57.

28.   Benedict XVI, 57 (emphasis added).

29.   Benedict XVI, Palm Sunday homily (March 16, 2008).

30.   "'My country, right or wrong,' is a thing that no patriot would think of saying except in a desperate case. It is like saying, 'My mother, drunk or sober'" (G. K. Chesterton, "A Defense of Patriotism," chap. 16 in *The Defendant* [Mineola, NY: Dover, 2012]).

31.   G.J. Goldberg, ed., "Part 7: The Siege and Destruction of
      Jerusalem March 70 - September 70," in *Chronology of the
      War According to Josephus*, available at josephus.org/.

32.   Charles J. Chaput, *Render Unto Caesar: Serving the Nation
      by Living Our Catholic Beliefs in Political Life* (New York:
      Doubleday, 2008), 218-219.

33.   Susan Hanssen, "Religion: A Public or a Private Right?,"
      Public Discourse, October 11, 2018, thepublicdiscourse.com/.

34.   Hanssen.

35.   Hanssen.

36.   Hanssen.

37.   Hanssen.

38.   John Adams to Massachusetts Militia, October 11, 1798, in
      John Adams and Charles Francis Adams, *The Works of John
      Adams, Second President of the United States*, vol. 9 (Boston:
      Little, Brown, and Company, 1854), 229.

39.   Richard R. Beeman, "Perspectives on the Constitution:
      A Republic, If You Can Keep It," *National Constitution
      Center*, constitutioncenter.org/.

40.   Hanssen, "Religion."

41.   Chaput, *Render Unto Caesar*, 30, original emphasis.

42.   Chaput, 219, original emphasis.

43.   Chaput, 219-220.

44.   Aquinas, *Summa Theologica* I-II.96.2.

45.   Aquinas.

46.   Aquinas, emphasis added.

Look

47. Aquinas, emphasis added.

48. Aquinas.

49. CCC 1806.

50. Michael Lerner, "Prohibition: Unintended Consequences," PBS (Public Broadcasting Service), pbs.org/.

51. Vatican II, *Gaudium et Spes* (December 7, 1965), 78, vatican.va/.

52. Vatican II.

53. Vatican II, 79.

54. Vatican II.

55. Vatican II.

56. Vatican II, 80.

57. Bernard E. Harcourt, "On Gun Registration, the NRA, Adolf Hitler, and Nazi Gun Laws: Exploding the Gun Culture Wars (A Call to Historians)," *Fordham Law Review* 73.2 (2004): 677.

58. "State to Disarm All Japs," *The Seattle Star*, February 21, 1942.

59. Specific passages from the CCC to support these bulleted points are provided throughout this chapter.

60. Aquinas, *Summa Theologica* II-II.66.7.

61. Aquinas.

62. John Paul II, *Memory and Identity: Conversations at the Dawn of a Millennium* (New York: Random House, 2005), 69–70.

63. John Paul II, 69-70.

64. John Paul II, Message for the 87th World Day of Migration, February 2, 2001, vatican.va/.

65. Benedict XVI, Message for the World Day of Migrants and Refugees, October 12, 2012, vatican.va/.

66. Benedict XVI.

67. Benedict XVI.

68. Stephen Herreid, commentary, *Catholic Vote*, February 28, 2017, catholicvote.org/.

69. Herreid.

70. Benedict XVI, 2012 Message.

71. William J. Clinton, Address Before a Joint Session of the Congress on the State of the Union, January 24, 1995, presidency.ucsb.edu/.

72. White House, President Bush's Plan for Comprehensive Immigration Reform, January 23, 2007, georgebush-whitehouse.archives.gov/.

73. White House, The Obama Administration's Government-Wide Response to Influx of Central American Migrants at the Southwest Border, August 1, 2014, obamawhitehouse.archives.gov/.

74. White House, Remarks by President Trump on the National Security and Humanitarian Crisis on Our Southern Border, February 15, 2019, whitehouse.gov/.

75. Kalhan Rosenblatt, "Will Trump's Border Wall Prevent Human Trafficking? Experts Aren't Sure," *NBC News*, April 26, 2017, nbcnews.com/.

76. White House, Remarks by President Trump in State of the Union Address, February 6, 2019, whitehouse.gov/.

77. Alex Horton, "Trump Keeps Calling the Southern Border Very Dangerous. It Is—But Not for Americans," *Washington Post*, January 20, 2018, washingtonpost.com/, emphasis added.

78.   Benedict XVI, 2012 Message.

79.   Benedict XVI.

80.   Francis, *Evangelii Gaudium* (November 24, 2014), 210, vatican.va/.

81.   Francis, *Christus Vivit* (March 24, 2019), 92, vatican.va/.

82.   Francis, 93, 94.

83.   Francis, *Gaudete et Exsultate* (March 19, 2018), 102, vatican.va/.

84.   Francis.

85.   Anthony Esolen, "Marriage Is Not a Water Fountain," *Public Discourse*, September 29, 2014, thepublicdiscourse.com/, emphasis added.

86.   Esolen.

87.   Esolen.

88.   Esolen.

89.   California Catholic Conference, Statement on Removal of St. Serra Statues in the State, June 22, 2020, cacatholic.org/.

90.   Francis, Homily at the Canonization of Blessed Fr. Junipero Serra, September 23, 2015, vatican.va/.

91.   Francis.

92.   Alejandra Molina, "Catholic Bishops Say Protesters 'Failed the Test' of History in Toppling Junipero Serra Statues," *Religion News Service*, June 23, 2020, religionnews.com/.

93.   "St. Junipero Serra Statue Torn Down in San Francisco," *Catholic News Agency*, June 20, 2020, catholicnewsagency.com/.

94.   John Paul II, *Centesimus Annus* (May 1, 1991), 37, vatican.va/.

95.   John Paul II.

96. John Paul II.

97. John Paul II, 38.

98. John Paul II, 38, emphasis added.

99. John Paul II, 38.

100. Francis, *Laudato Si'* (May 24, 2015), 44-45.

101. Francis, 61.

102. Francis, 214.

103. Francis, 164.

104. Francis.

105. Francis.

106. Francis, 173.

107. Francis.

108. Francis, 174.

109. Francis, 175.

110. Francis, 178.

111. Francis, 179.

112. Francis, 142.

113. Francis, 144, emphasis added.

114. Francis, 179.

115. Francis, 211.

116. Francis.

117. Francis, 214.

118. Francis, 211.

119. Francis, 213.

120. Francis, 61.

121. Francis, 180.

122. John Paul II, *Dies Domini* ("The Lord's Day") (May 31, 1998), 11.

123. National Institutes of Health, "Greek Medicine: The Hippocratic Oath," *US National Library of Medicine*, February 7, 2012, nlm.nih.gov/; see also N. S. Gill, "Is It Myth That 'First Do No Harm' Is in the Hippocratic Oath?," *ThoughtCo*, October 19, 2019, thoughtco.com/.

124. To view the manuscript online, see Vatican Library, "Urb Greca 64," *DIGIVATLIB* (DVL), digi.vatlib.it/.

125. See Maureen Condic, *When Does Human Life Begin: A Scientific Perspective* (Thornwood, NY: Westchester Institute for Ethics and the Human Person, 2008).

126. "National Right to Life Pleased with Drop in U.S. Abortion Rate," National Right to Life, September 18, 2019, nrlc.org/.

127. John Paul II, *Evangelium Vitae* (March 25, 1995), 66.

128 New revision of number 2267 of the *Catechism of the Catholic Church* on the death penalty – Rescriptum "ex Audentia SS.mi", 02.08.2018, press.vatican.va/.

129. Joseph Ratzinger, "Worthiness to Receive Holy Communion: General Principles," July 2004, ewtn.com/, 3.

130. Ratzinger, 2.

131. Jonathon van Maren, "Atheists in Praise of Christianity?," *The Stream*, May 19, 2020, stream.org.

132 Epistle to Diognetus, chapter 7.

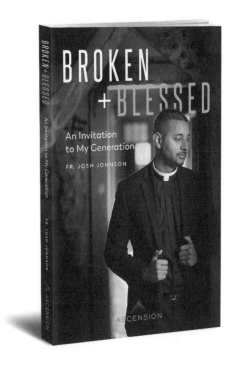

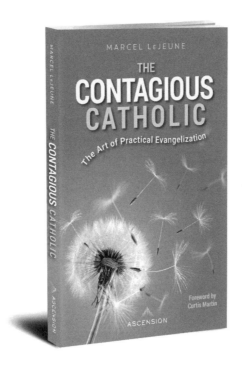

Scripture—the Original **Smart Guide** to Life

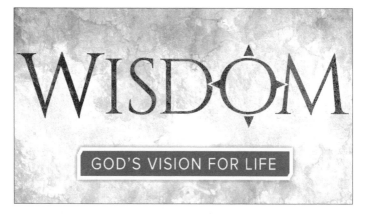

WISD♦M

GOD'S VISION FOR LIFE

An Eight-Part Study by Jeff Cavins and Thomas Smith

Drawing on the wisdom literature of the Bible—Proverbs, Wisdom, Sirach, and Ecclesiastes—***Wisdom: God's Vison for Life*** teaches you how to actively seek out sound guidance and increase your sense of peace while navigating your daily life. Learn how to gather and grow in biblical wisdom and experience the joy and security it brings to your relationships, friendships, finances, and sense of well-being.